MW00914071

FIORI GIOVANNI

DEFY YOUR DESTINY

MAKE YOUR MOST PAINFUL WALK YOUR MOST TRIUMPHANT JOURNEY

Defy Your Destiny is an incredible and moving story about one woman's resilience, grit, determination and choice to survive and thrive, despite overwhelming odds, challenges and suffering. 'Inspirational and empowering' doesn't even begin to describe Fiori's incredible memoir. A must-read for every woman, man and child, to truly understand how ordinary people are capable of the most extraordinary things.

Rabia Siddique—International humanitarian, professional speaker, and best-selling author of *Equal Justice*

Fiori's harrowing and inspirational life story personifies courage against insurmountable odds, including war, death threats, abuse, racism and sexism. An ordinary person would have succumbed. Fiori demonstrates, time and time again through her story, that she is extraordinary. From a teenage boat-person refugee, to building a new life in diverse cultures across Africa, Europe and finally Australia, she now guides and mentors leading corporate achievers.

Fiori's story is transformational. Maximise your life with Fiori's blueprint, which you are holding now. There is power in this story. Plug in, turn on, take action and never give up. Everyone should be so lucky to have Fiori Giovanni in their life.

Brian James—National and international award-winning journalist, and radio and TV presenter

Fiori Giovanni's story of survival demonstrates that the path out of almost impossible circumstances is built on a foundation of courage, determination and resilience.

David Pougher—Opinion Editor, Herald Sun and Sunday Herald Sun

---

A deeply powerful and complex personal story expressed thoughtfully and with rare candour. Fiori's openness to life and generosity radiate throughout the text, providing insights that are both immediate and universal. Her ability to draw lessons from her past to define her own future, provides an invaluable example applicable to readers, irrespective of their unique circumstances.

Emil Davityan—Co-Founder, CEO of Bluedot Innovation

Absolutely enrapturing. From the minute you open the book, you will struggle to put it down. Fiori takes you on a journey, her journey—one where you find yourself empathising, crying with her, smiling unwittingly, feeling fear for her, and ultimately rooting for her with a sense of empowerment along the way. This book was pure enjoyment to read. Highly recommended.

Kel Ho—Senior Marketing Consultant

First published in 2019 by SAGT Pty Ltd

Melbourne Australia

www.fiorigiovanni.com

Copyright © 2019 Fiori Giovanni

All rights reserved. Except as permitted under the Australian Copyright Act 1968, no part of this publication may be reproduced, stored in a retrieval system, or transmitted in any form or by any means, electronic, mechanical, photocopying, recording or otherwise, without prior written permission. All enquiries should be made to the author.

Author: Fiori Giovanni

Title: *Defy Your Destiny–Make your most painful walk your most triumphant journey*

ISBN: 9780648469100

Subjects: Self-development – Memoir

Publishing services: www.bevryanpublishing.com

Disclaimer

The material in this publication is of the nature of general comment only, and does not represent professional advice. It is not intended to provide specific guidance for particular circumstances and it should not be relied on as the basis of any decision to take action or not take action on any matter which it covers. Readers should obtain professional advice where appropriate, before making any such decision. To the maximum extent permitted by law, the author and publisher disclaim all responsibility and liability to any person, arising directly or indirectly from any person taking or not taking action based on the information in this publication.

Note: The events in this book are factual. However, to protect the identity and safety of individuals, the names of people and their relationship(s) to me have sometimes been changed.

This book is dedicated to my beloved brother,

Amanuel, as well as the many voiceless people

who have lost their lives in search of freedom.

TABLE OF CONTENTS

Map of Eritrea, a northeast African country on the Red Sea coast. It shares borders with Ethiopia, Sudan and Djibouti. (Dr Fred Hollows from Australia was responsible for extensive sight-restorative surgery in Eritrea.)

CHAPTER ONE

MY AFRICAN CHILDHOOD:
SUNSHINE AND RAIN

Our destiny isn't one big destination

at some specified point of life.

It's the choices we make at the

many stops on our life path.

Senait, a beautiful girl in our town, was twelve years old on her wedding day.

She stood still and quietly as her friends and family chatted and fussed around her, dressing her in white Christian wedding clothes and draping her in blankets.

I caught a glimpse of her beautiful eyes before her head was completely covered.

They were brown like coffee.

Curved like almonds.

Sparkling like diamonds.

But once the blankets were cast over her head, the sparkle extinguished.

Senait was gone.

In her place was a faceless white flag, surrendering.

The young man she was about to marry was Aron. It was her destiny to marry him because her father made the arrangements long before Senait could even walk and talk.

For many Eritrean parents, the ultimate life goal is for their children to marry early, and to have babies quickly, even if they are practically babies themselves. Some girls in the villages marry as young as eight years old when their tiny bodies are barely buds on a tree.

Senait met her husband for the first time during the ceremony, though the term 'meet' is a bit of a stretch. It was impossible for Senait to actually *see* Aron because the blankets covered her face, and she permanently bowed her head.

During the ceremony though, Senait *did* hold Aron's hand while being blessed by Eritrean elders, friends, family, and church leaders. I wondered what the touch of his skin told her. A nice man with soft hands? A rough man who did manual work?

Hard to say, but the first time Senait actually laid eyes on Aron was when he lay *on* her that night, at his parents' home.

I imagined what he saw when he looked at her face.

Eyes brown like coffee.

Curved like almonds.

Completely filled with terror.

Years later I found out that Senait's wedding night was a confusing, frightening night. A night that flowed into an endless stream of similar nights, until sex became an uncomfortable kind of normal.

Sex didn't involve any kind of protection, so Senait was pregnant immediately at the age of twelve, and had several children before she reached the age of twenty.

If the agony of having babies while so young wasn't enough, Aron beat her regularly, which was lawful. And cheated on her often, which was common.

Not surprisingly, Senait escaped back to our village sometimes.

She'd walk for two hours in the blazing heat with one child on her back, one in her arms, and the weight of the world on her shoulders.

Her parents denied her desperate pleas to allow her to stay. They'd give her a meal and send her on her way. She'd stand up, on raw, tired feet, to make the long hobble back to hell.

Her parents weren't cruel people; they simply didn't know any differently.

Senait belonged to her husband.

She was less, he was more.

He was superior, she was his servant.

She submitted, he enslaved.

That was her destiny.

That's the destiny for many Eritrean girls, and sadly, the inequality is evident from the moment a baby is born.

In my town of Maidamu, babies were birthed at home. The births were brutal, often with either the baby or mother dying, and tragically, sometimes both. In my own family, three of my siblings were stillborn.

Deaths were such a high probability during childbirth that when a healthy newborn baby greeted the world with a wail, it was cause for laughter and excitement. The family and relatives made a joyous, celebratory chanting sound, which also served to announce the gender.

For a boy, there were seven chants.

For a girl, three.

And so it was, from the time a girl took her first breath, she was deemed less than half as important as her brothers.

That's the sad reality for females in Eritrea.

It was no different for my own cousin, Almaz, who I loved and admired.

She was always like a princess to me, so tall and graceful, with flowing brown hair like a sea of endless, desert dunes.

When her Christian marriage to Dani was arranged, I was horrified.

I never expected to see this happen to someone in my own family.

It was a surprise, and yet later in life, I would realise it wasn't surprising at all.

It was 1989, when the war between Eritrea and neighbouring Ethiopia was heating up, as Eritrea fought for independence—a brutal and bloody war that lasted thirty long years from 1961 to 1991, resulting in thousands of casualties and displaced people.

My cousin Almaz was stunningly beautiful. Her body was developing rapidly, and she looked much older than her twelve years. If unmarried, she risked becoming an Eritrean soldier, or worse, being used as a sex slave by the enemy, the Ethiopian soldiers.

Although I was only four when Almaz was married, I remember how sad and passive she looked on her wedding day.

Rather than fighting her destiny, she simultaneously accepted and mourned it.

The families didn't mourn though.

The wedding was a loud, joyous occasion. There was dancing, music, food, and many jugs of *siwa*, which is the strong home-brewed Eritrean alcohol.

At celebrations like weddings, some people were able to momentarily forget their everyday worries. Not most parents though. Most parents worried about the safety of their children constantly. They saw how war brought out the worst in people, especially the soldiers.

One of my earliest traumatic memories was watching an Eritrean female literally being sliced in half and then raped by an Ethiopian soldier. The vision of this gruesome atrocity haunts me to this day.

On another occasion, I saw two Ethiopian soldiers cut off the penis of our older neighbour and play with it like a ball. Again, a memory I simply can't forget.

These are just two examples of dozens of horrendous acts I witnessed. All these hideous acts were done under the banner of war, but carried out for personal pleasure. The barbaric treatment was widespread.

Many Eritreans were so sick of the inhumanity and unfairness that some parents *encouraged* their children to fight in the war against the Ethiopians, despite the risks.

Death was not a deterrent. If their children died during battle, the parents felt equal measures of grief and pride—grief because their children had perished, pride because their children died defending beautiful Eritrea.

Some of my family members and friends thought differently, though, especially my Uncle Debesay. (He wasn't my uncle by blood, but he was such a close family friend that we treated him like one.)

We all spent much time together, which meant I got to know his family well, particularly his two fun-loving sons, Tesfay and Flimon. I was much younger than them, but they loved having a 'little sister' around. They'd play lots of games with me, and always kept me entertained and safe.

To Uncle Debesay, war was never a path to greatness or peace, just a road lined with rotting corpses and decaying dreams.

His goal was to keep his family alive, which is why he did something quite extraordinary and dangerous.

To protect his boys, he sent Tesfay and Flimon to hide with family members in another city. (If the authorities found out, Uncle Debesay could be imprisoned or killed.)

Their departure happened under a veil of secrecy; in fact, even the boys didn't know they were leaving.

I remember wondering where they'd disappeared to. They were always here and there, but never *nowhere*.

I was so puzzled.

I asked their mum, Aunty Lemlem, but she always changed the subject.

The village seemed empty without them. Yet, full of secrets.

These secrets rolled from place to place like clouds before a storm.

I witnessed that storm crack and thunder before my very eyes during the dark, early hours of one Sunday morning. There was a knock on Uncle Debesay's door. (I was sleeping at their house, as I sometimes did, to keep Aunty Lemlem company.) My uncle answered the door to see two soldiers standing outside.

'Sir, please accompany us,' they said.

By the look on Uncle Debesay's face, he didn't want to, but had to comply. To resist would mean death or injury.

He dressed in front of them while Aunty Lemlem looked on in shock.

As he left with the soldiers, Aunty Lemlem sobbed quietly on her bed.

I lay there, not knowing what to do, what to say.

The whole village found out about the events through a neighbour the next morning. Bad news spreads like a disease in villages.

My parents rushed over, worried senseless about me.

When they saw I was fine, their relief turned to sadness for Aunty Lemlem.

There were many people in the home. In fact, a stream of nearly forty were passing through, sharing their condolences. The number of people reflected the gravity of the situation.

When someone had been taken by soldiers, it was rare for them ever to return. No one knew whether Uncle Debesay would be tortured, killed, or put in prison for years; all scenarios were possible.

The thought of him gone, and possibly being hurt or killed, made me feel sick inside.

Aunty Lemlem shook with worry for days, and yet, she still needed to care for her three-year-old son, Henock. I could see her going through the motions, even though her forehead crinkled more and more with each passing moment.

A few days after everything happened, as Henock walked alongside his mother, he said, 'Can Aunty Helen walk into the house with us, Mumma?'

Aunty Helen was my mum, and he wanted her to walk into the house with them because the void left by his father's and brothers' absence was so vast.

His mum cried and hugged him. 'Yes my son. Yes, we can do that.'

They came to our home and made the request.

My mum agreed enthusiastically and also hugged Henock tightly.

Mum happily went to their house that night, and five more nights after that until Henock was emotionally ready to walk through the door without her.

It was a beautiful example of how it takes a village to raise a child.

In this case, it wasn't just a village raising a child—it was a village supporting the child's mother as well. Aunty Lemlem drew on the strength of this village, visiting family and friends often, including my mum.

In fact, Aunty Lemlem frequently stopped by the grocery store we owned.

When I'd peek inside, I'd see my mum and Aunty Lemlem crying. I didn't realise it then, but my mum wasn't just crying because of Uncle Debesay; she was crying for the loss of justice in our country—that a man must make the most painful decision to tear his family apart in order to keep his sons safe. Then, be punished for it.

When Aunty Lemlem left the store, I'd ask my mum why they were crying.

'We've been cutting onions,' she'd say.

Yum, invisible curry, my favourite!

Seeing my mum so miserable, I had no interest in playing outside anymore. I stayed near her because staying close stopped her from crying.

When Mum realised I was staying inside all the time, she started giving me tasks to do. Small ones at first, then bigger ones.

Mum liked that I picked up instructions quickly, and used my common sense.

She liked that I'd try to solve problems, and stay calm even when things weren't going right.

I helped for many weeks.

As time went on, I noticed Aunty Lemlem didn't stop by as often. She had learned to live again, although always under a cloud of sadness.

My few weeks of helping at the grocery store turned into months. Within a year, at a very young age, I was running it on my own without Mum even being there. I stocked shelves, helped customers, took money, and basically did everything I was taught to do, and additional things I wasn't.

It wasn't a big deal to me, but Mum bragged and boasted about my work ethic and character to neighbours. She'd say, 'Fiori is an old soul in a child's body. She says the wisest things!'

But actually, I think Henock, Aunty Lemlem's son, was far wiser.

He had a calm, sensible way about him. Sometimes when I'd see him deep in contemplation, I wished that Uncle Debesay would return home *just for him*. I wanted Henock's happiness more than I wanted my own.

My one, ongoing dream for Henock was to feel peace and protection in his father's presence again.

And in two years' time, my dream came true.

By some miracle, Uncle Debesay was alive.

He'd been in prison and returned home in one, thinner piece.

Aunty Lemlem's happiness burst forth in chants that even the heavens could hear.

I remember the first time I saw Uncle Debesay after his return. It *did* seem like a dream. Everything moved in slow motion.

It was him, really him.

I hugged him so tightly I thought I'd break his body as much as *my* heart had broken in his absence.

He was handsome still, but his body seemed weary. He said very little to me about his time in prison, and I asked few questions.

The lines on his face scrawled sentences I dared not even try to read. He was home, and that's what mattered.

I was just grateful.

A place where I *did* ask questions, a *lot* of questions, was school.

My formal education began in 1991 at the age of six, and school was a place where my eternal hunger for knowledge could be satisfied.

I listened carefully and applied myself studiously. The results reflected in my marks where I often topped the class, or even the entire school.

My brother Amanuel started with me at this elementary school, and we completed grades one to five there.

When it was time for grade six, Amanuel and I moved to Araza to attend a good junior school. My parents arranged a place for us to stay from Monday to Friday, and on Friday afternoons we'd return to our home in Maidamu.

During that time, I naturally spent a lot of time with Amanuel, and I began seeing him as more than just my little brother.

He was almost like an angel.

His aura was drenched in calmness.

His smile sparkled with serenity.

His wisdom flowed deeply.

His devoutness shone brightly.

Had I not been so busy in the past, I would have paid more attention to him. Now, I regretted losing time around Amanuel's positivity and insight.

I felt so fortunate having him as my brother. And yet, I wondered how we were even related?

He was still and accepting.

I was outspoken and fearless.

He was a leaf in the breeze.

I was a buffalo in a stampede, charging in the *opposite* direction, away from common thought and my looming destinies.

But although so different in many ways, we sometimes were like one person, thinking the same thoughts and finishing each other's sentences.

And I could talk to him about *anything*.

I would often share my dream of moving away from Eritrea one day, of fleeing the never-ending war and violence.

But war didn't affect Amanuel in the same way. He accepted the world for what it was, and tried to make it better in his own peaceful way.

He made no plans.

He was in no hurry.

He was happy to just live in the moment. And right now, that meant being a student. Being told what to do.

I was a student too, but I did *not* like being told what to do, how to think, what to believe.

Mostly, I was endlessly curious and asked so many questions. The students saw this as a positive attribute and often voted me for leadership positions, which I relished.

But the teachers saw my questions in a different way.

They thought I was being rude and disrespectful.

Rather than embracing my enquiring mind and using my questions as a launch pad for discussion and debate, they silenced me. To do this, they'd resort to physical punishment.

There were three main punishments at my school, and I had the great honour of winning this trifecta many times.

The 'light' punishment involved kneeling on the hard floor for the duration of the class, which was around an hour. (This punishment might *seem* light, but when you must kneel still without shifting or swaying, your knees eventually become like two hotplates, burning with pain.)

For the harsher punishment, I'd kneel for the duration of the class again, but this time outside in the sun while holding a large, heavy rock. This was a triple whammy because my knees would burn, my hands and shoulders would ache, and my body would bake in the blazing sun. After an hour I'd be a sweating, throbbing mess of quivering flesh.

But, it was better than the third, and worst, punishment.

The third punishment involved kneeling outside holding a heavy rock, but this time it was *all* day, and at the end of that day, I'd be beaten with a stick.

Here's what made it worse.

I was beaten often, so in many cases the scratches and bruises from the previous day were still fresh and raw. This meant the stick felt like barbed wire. Barbed wire that lashed and thrashed at open wounds and unanswered questions.

Despite the pain, I was never broken or silenced.

I continued asking the same questions.

Why must girls get married to a stranger at such a young age?

Why must girls become mothers and wives, and nothing else?

Why must girls support their husband's dreams rather than pursuing their own dreams?

Why must there be so much violence and cruelty?

Why is peace so hard for our country to enjoy?

Why can't countries work together?

Why can't there be give and take?

Why must we aim to win at all costs, despite the casualties?

I asked these questions not to be rude or disrespectful, but because I desperately wanted to know the answers.

From where I was standing (or kneeling), none of it made sense.

I was totally confused.

I also was not interested in being silenced, no matter how sharp the stick or raw my wounds.

I took my punishment with pride. My stripes and welts were like ribbons after a race, medals after a marathon. (Many years later, I would watch *Forrest Gump* and feel a solid kinship with his character. He ran and ran through life toward a destiny of his choosing, never giving up, no matter what life threw at him.)

The school punishment, as it turns out, would be a metaphor for my life: challenging the world, kneeling alone, carrying problems like heavy stones, grimacing with pain, but always rising stronger than before.

Amanuel hated seeing me bruised and beaten.

'Fiori, stop asking so many questions!' he'd beg.

But he didn't realise the impossibility of his request. It was like asking me to stop breathing.

He couldn't understand, because he looked at the world with a sense of acceptance, contentment, and compassion.

Whenever I complained about cruelty and injustices, he'd say, 'Fiori, you need to put your faith in God. With God, whatever is meant to be, will be.'

He loved God devoutly, as did I, but his love flowed through him like a humming stream.

Calmness made him the perfect counsellor, and as such, he always held up a mirror to my anger. He grounded me, and was a voice of reason in a noisy, chaotic country.

He was loving and affectionate to a fault, though. His gentleness, innocence, and sense of charity made him a target for bullies and scammers ... unless *I* knew about it. I was a lioness around him, fighting on his behalf regularly, either with total strangers or even with our parents.

I tried my best to protect Amanuel from everyone and everything, always, and at all costs. It's what anyone would do for their soulmate, their best friend.

But I knew I had to protect myself too, and work toward a different future. In building a better future for myself, I knew I'd be building a better future for Amanuel.

That's why my life needed to take a detour.

Away from Amanuel.

Away from school.

Away from my destiny.

This is how it happened.

———————⇒➤●◄⇐———————

During my first year of junior school, at eleven years old, one of my teachers was a Catholic nun. She was the only teacher who didn't fear my questions, so I liked her instantly.

One day I asked, 'Don't you hate wearing the same uniform every single day?'

'Women change their hairstyles and clothes every day to please their men,' she replied. 'God doesn't expect this of me. I please no one but God.'

Her answer danced in the air.

I could barely speak as it spun around me.

It was like the heavens opened up and drizzled glorious sunshine upon me.

It was as if a giant lightbulb flashed brightly above my head.

To me, she'd said the most Godly, earth-shattering statement in the history of the world.

Her belief aligned with my own thinking. Women did *not* have to live their lives pleasing men.

I decided, there and then—I wanted to be a nun.

The idea of living my life to please my God, and *no man*, was beyond exhilarating.

I couldn't wait to tell my parents!

But when I shared the exciting news with them, they were far from happy.

'No daughter of mine is going to be a nun!' Dad yelled. 'We are Christian Orthodox, not Catholic!'

I dug my heels in.

I wasn't backing down.

My beautiful dad was reaping what he'd sown. All my life he'd constantly built up my self-esteem and confidence. He had always told me how intelligent I was, how I was destined for great things. He had told me I was worthy, and that my worth could move mountains.

Now, I was at the top of that mountain, standing my ground.

We argued back and forth for hours.

For every question, I had an answer.

For every problem, I had a solution.

For every threat, I had a shrug.

Finally, he relented. 'Fine, if you insist on being a nun, change your surname first, because you won't be my daughter anymore.'

'If you're so embarrassed,' I snapped, 'change your own name. I'm keeping mine.'

And I did.

I immediately proceeded to the bus stop, where I boarded a bus to the Catholic nuns' camp in Keren.

———⇒➤●◄⇐———

The bus ride to Keren was nine hours away.

I could feel every inch of the journey because the pothole-filled roads meant the trip was a series of bumps, jumps, and thumps.

We were thrown this way and that, but the prospect of broken bones was a small price to pay. I would have endured another nine uncomfortable hours if it meant heading toward a destiny of my choosing.

Thankfully, though, I eventually arrived that evening, and in one piece.

At the camp I was greeted by a nun. She was wearing a light blue robe typical of the order of Saint Anna.

Her welcome was brief, and she immediately led me through several doors.

I saw two big bedrooms, each housing around sixteen beds.

I also saw an adjacent room that had two big dining tables.

My heart fluttered.

In this building I would be eating, sleeping, praying, learning. *Living.*

She pointed to the bedroom and said, 'It's an early start tomorrow; get some sleep.'

I crept in. The other girls were busy dreaming.

After the uncomfortable bus ride, that's exactly what I wanted to do too.

I fell asleep fast, and it seemed was woken up just as quickly.

When I looked at the time, it was 4:30 a.m.

Okay, that's early.

That's *very* early.

With bleary eyes, I followed what the other girls were doing.

They got out of bed and knelt down to pray.

I stumbled to my knees and shared a Bible with the girl next to me, who gave me a fleeting smile.

I read the prayers everyone else was reading. We did this for around fifteen minutes. From there, the day moved quickly, and looked something like this.

At 4:45 a.m. I took a quick shower and got dressed.

At 5:00 a.m. I was told to do some cleaning tasks by a nun. My tasks were a mix of sweeping, mopping and gardening.

At 6:00 a.m. we went to church for more prayers.

At 7:00 a.m. we ate breakfast and changed into our school uniforms.

At 7:30 a.m. we attended lessons at a nearby school.

At 1:00 p.m. school finished, and we returned to the camp to have free time until 3:00 p.m.

At 3:00 p.m. we started the afternoon routine, which involved chores, reading the Bible, learning religious songs, praying, and eventually eating.

At night we fell into bed. Like everyone else, my brain was mush and my body was exhausted.

I assumed the next day would be slightly different, but every single day was a carbon copy of the day before.

Prior to coming to the camp, I knew there'd be a routine, even a strict routine.

I knew there'd be rules.

Within the routine and rules though, I was expecting moments of discussion and enlightenment.

But no, everything was robotic and rehearsed.

The same prayers.

The same lessons.

The same spoon-feeding of information that was only for absorption, not discussion.

The mechanical nature of the day seemed to leech me of all enthusiasm.

I ended up doing everything without care or conviction, which I realised didn't matter to anyone.

The camp turned out to be a mindless existence that neither fed my mind nor satisfied my soul. I had more meaningful conversations with God quietly, before I joined the camp, than I did surrounded by nuns.

Furthermore, the nuns were 'servants of God' in name only.

They scrutinised and criticised our every move, dragging us down rather than building us up, forcing passiveness rather than inciting passion.

When I tried to generate a discussion about something, I was silenced.

I'd jumped from the pot into the fire!

I kept hoping things would change. I really *wanted* them to change. But after thirteen months, I realised this would be my life.

Finally, I thought to myself, 'This is bullshit!'

I couldn't take it any longer.

Much to my father's delight, I headed back to high school, living with Amanuel in Mendefera.

I loved seeing Amanuel again.

When I described to him life at the camp, he thought it sounded amazing. It was his type of life! He would have loved being a sponge, soaking up every piece of information without question or quandary.

I had been restless at the camp, and truth be told, I was restless in Mendefera too.

As much as I loved being with Amanuel, within a year I yearned to move on. My teenage hormones kicked in, and I wanted to get as far away from my parents as possible. I wanted to be my own person, fully. I was sick of swimming upstream along with all the other salmon.

So I made the decision to head back to Keren. Even though I didn't like the nuns' camp, I liked the city. It was bustling and exciting. And most of all, it was far away.

My parents weren't pleased, and of course, neither was Amanuel. But they all knew that once I set my mind on something, I had to do it.

They wouldn't stop me.

They *couldn't* stop me.

———————————⋗●⋖———————————

In Keren, I continued going to high school during the day, and worked outside of school hours.

Without work, I felt empty and unfulfilled. I also liked earning money, and I *loved* being independent.

My parents were proud of my desire to support myself, but they were not happy about the type of work I did.

In fact, they were furious.

I worked as a servant for a family, so I was like a maid. My father was unhappy because servants are considered the lowest class in Eritrea—unimportant and insignificant. In his eyes, my decision to become a servant, particularly when our own family had servants of our own, brought incredible shame on the family.

It wasn't my intention to bring shame; I just wanted to work. I didn't feel I was better or above anyone else, so why *wouldn't* I work as a maid?

And besides, if I was outraged that females were treated as less than men, how could I dare treat servants as less than me?

I ignored the outcry from my parents. I cleaned everything from toys to toilets, and I did it with pride.

This was a defining point in my life because I was defying a particular part of my destiny.

I was defying the class code that dictates who is less and who is more, and the types of choices I should make as a result.

I was defying *how* I should earn money.

I was defying the *type* of work I should do.

I no longer floundered in crowded waters along with everyone else. I swam in a different stream where the waves felt warm and revitalising.

It was there, in those clear, refreshing waters, that I started thinking deeply about life, about freedom, about my hopes and dreams. About what was right. What was wrong. What I stood for.

About my destiny.

I thought a *lot* about my destiny.

I started answering the questions that teachers punished me for asking.

I started solving puzzles that had confused and mystified me for so long.

I started seeing everything with a dazzling clarity.

With time and space, I worked it out for myself.

I found the answers *within* me.

I realised my destiny wasn't one big destination at some specified point in my life—it was the choices I made at the many stops on my life *path*.

Each time I defied my destiny, I was getting a taste of mouth-watering, addictive freedom.

I was being awakened by freedom.

Exploring freedom.

Understanding freedom.

Freedom, to me, meant not being chained to people, places, purposes, positions—either the chains I was born with, or the ones I voluntarily placed around my own neck.

Freedom was a voyage that took twists and turns over velvet pastures and jagged rocks, through curtains of rainbows and sheets of hail.

It was the eternal, bottomless well of my life.

A well filled with goals of great love, great wealth, great fortune, and great energy.

With freedom, I was the highest form of whoever I was meant to be, on any given day, at any given moment. Free from anger and filled with self-love. No better or worse than anyone else.

I realised that understanding freedom would help me continually defy my destiny.

I also realised I would need every *ounce* of that understanding possible, because my most feared and hated destiny was just around the corner.

My wedding day.

CHAPTER TWO

REALISATION: BREAKING THE CHAINS

Open the door to accountability,

and you break the chains of misery.

I returned home to Maidamu from Keren, for what was meant to be a relaxing visit.

But it became stressful, fast.

While sitting at the table one day looking out the window, my father told me it was time for me to be married, and that a twenty-five-year-old husband had been chosen for me.

I froze.

It felt as though a creeping shadow, one that had lurked near me since birth, finally stood tall, walking into my body, devouring my soul.

The world had instantly changed.

The sky, so blue and vast, looked more like a suffocating blanket of smoke, rising high to the heavens from my burning, breaking heart.

The rays of light that had previously beamed in instantly changed to solid, black bars.

And the ribbons of clouds that blew with the breeze curled casually into nooses.

The world didn't change for my dad though. It continued to turn in its slow, usual way, and I was expected to turn slowly and robotically with it.

'Fiori, you're twelve years old now,' he said. 'That's the marrying age for girls in our village. The man I've picked for you has achieved great success in his trading business. He's respectful to his parents and is admired throughout the community. I've also heard he's quite good looking!'

I dragged my eyes away from the window. 'You haven't even met him?'

Delighted that I'd finally spoken, my father smiled. 'It's not necessary. He comes highly recommended from people we trust. Of course, I have other options in grooms, but I believe this man is the best for you.'

'What about my education?'

'If you want to stay at school so badly, he might understand and let you stay on. But of course, once you're married you'll probably want to focus on having children and being part of his business.'

My brain seemed to erupt.

He *might* understand that I need to go to school?

He may *let* me continue with my education?

Was I in a nightmare?

Would I wake up and see my *real* father? The man who'd built up my confidence and self-esteem my entire life? Who had told me I could run whole countries?

Reading my mind, Dad said, 'It's the norm, Fiori. Most girls can't wait to get married; it's the highlight of their lives. Marriage will give you independence from your family. Don't you want that?'

'I'm already independent,' I snapped. 'I've already made my own choices and lived away from you and Mum. A man won't give me independence. He'll lock me in a marital cage at twelve!'

'You're being dramatic, Fiori!' Dad huffed. 'I don't think you realise how lucky you are. Because of our standing in the community and our business ventures, you have interest from the most sought-after men in the villages. The older you get, the less choice in husbands you'll have. You'll be left out. All the girls will be married but you.'

Yes, all the girls.

I often talked to *all the girls*.

At school, when all the girls squealed with delight at the thought of getting married, I inwardly shrieked with terror. This made me feel like a stranger in my own village.

My own country.

My own culture.

In quiet moments, I wondered whether my arrival to beautiful Africa was one of heaven's greatest administrative errors!

I wasn't like the other girls, and I was becoming more *unlike* them as the days went by.

I had questioned and defied certain destinies already.

I had tasted freedom.

I *was* different, so I certainly wasn't going to react passively, like all the other girls.

Instead, I argued with my dad.

I argued every moment of every day.

I didn't bother appealing to my mother because my father was head of the household. He was the decision maker. (I preferred talking to Dad anyway, because he always treated me like an adult, valued my opinions, and rigorously debated with me on many issues.)

And he was debating with me now, more than ever.

He *had* to. I was incessant.

'Dad, you say I'm destined for greatness. What greatness can I find when I am the property of a man?'

'You will use your greatness to seek permission,' he said, 'to keep achieving your dreams.'

'That's like putting a spider under a cup and asking it to spin a large web,' I replied. 'I hold so many leadership positions at school, and yet you want me to become a follower, to take orders from a man? You told me I was different from all the other girls, but now you want me to conform?'

He faltered. 'Well, you can make your marriage different, because *you* are different.'

It was a lie.

He knew it.

I knew it.

So he changed the direction of the debate by voicing a complaint. 'No other girl I've known has argued with their parents this much.'

He was right. I'd never witnessed other girls speaking their minds.

I'd never seen examples of women defying their destiny.

I didn't own a television or radio or receive newspapers, any of which would have provided examples of female empowerment or glimpses of a better life.

In the absence of role models, I relied on two traits my father noticed and nurtured in me: instinct and logic. If he had known that one day I would use these traits to defy both him and my destiny, he may not have been so encouraging.

I shrugged my shoulders. 'I'm just doing what you taught me. I'm standing up for what's right. I'm not defying you, just the future you're forcing upon me.'

Dad mumbled something and walked away. As usual, our argument had gone around in dizzying, unresolved circles.

We argued constantly.

Sometimes we'd be debating each other for days without a break, sometimes weeks, and sadly, even months.

At times I was so exhausted from all the arguing, I briefly *entertained* the idea of getting married.

Then I'd think of Senait.

She still regularly escaped back to our village.

I'd sometimes see her. The beautiful, lively princess had gone. Sorrow hung in bags under each dull and vacant eye.

Admittedly, not all girls experienced abusive and miserable marriages like Senait.

I knew of a few girls who'd married caring boys and lived pleasant lives.

But to me, 'pleasant' was just a few steps up from unhappiness. Even if my husband was Prince Charming, I had no interest in being swept up and cared for. I wanted to walk my own path, on my own two feet, toward my own dreams.

Dad wasn't having any of it, though.

I assumed my constant arguments would persuade and prevail, convince and cajole.

But one night as I lay in bed, it dawned on me that I possibly wouldn't be able to talk my way out of this. That I'd *actually* have to get married.

The night instantly became blacker.

And the blackness swallowed me whole.

It filled my mind with dark, damaging thoughts.

Being a wife at twelve years old was no way to live.

No way to live at all.

No!

Just no!

If I have to get married, then I don't want to live. I'd rather die than succumb to my destiny. I'd rather endure a painful early end, than a bitter beginning, and an agonising, prolonged middle.

Such thoughts propelled me forward, to fearless, shadowy places.

The next day I visited an older cousin and offloaded my grievances.

I felt relieved to let my churning thoughts tumble out like dirty laundry.

I wasn't there just to vent, though—I wanted guidance too.

'I need your help,' I said. 'Can you show me how to tie a noose?'

Her eyebrows turned into launching rockets. 'What? No! Why would you ask such a question? You're not seriously thinking about ... are you?!'

'What choice do I have? I know you think I'm crazy, but I think everyone else is crazy for thinking it's normal to be married at twelve!'

She firmly shook her head. 'Fiori, forget it.'

I decided to take a different approach. I laughed. 'You believed me? I was kidding! As if I'd kill myself.'

Her eyes narrowed suspiciously. 'Promise?'

'Promise,' I lied.

I put on such a convincing show that I even talked her into demonstrating how to tie the noose anyway.

She was so gullible.

Later, I found out *I* was the gullible one. She'd shown me an incorrect way. A way that would have led to nothing but a scraped knee and a bruised ego.

Still, when I look back, it's devastating that I even contemplated suicide at such a young age. But death seemed like the only option at the time. Dying on my own terms, once and for all, rather than dying slowly over the course of a 'life' time, seemed like the only humane path.

When I returned home from my cousin's house, I calmly and firmly made this announcement to my parents: 'If I'm forced to marry, I'll kill myself. The food you're preparing for my wedding can be used for my funeral because I'll be dead.'

My parents stood quietly for a moment staring at me.

My back was straight, and my eyes were steely. I was so determined and so defiant that my parents realised I was serious about my threat.

They looked at each other, then back at me again.

Eventually, reluctantly, they gave in.

Within days the wedding was cancelled.

My parents were quiet for weeks, and I hated seeing them unhappy. It was hard living with their disappointment, but it was easier than living with my misery.

Ever the tenacious man though, my father still checked periodically to see whether I'd changed my mind. Or he'd inform me of other interested suitors. The names of the men changed from month to month, but my answer was always the same: 'No thanks.'

With the burden of an impending marriage off my shoulders, I was able to focus on school again: learning, interacting, growing, and maturing. *This* was my life from now on. A life of education and empowerment.

I defied another destiny.

It was a small step toward the many paths of my choosing.

Or, so I thought. I had won one battle, but another was just around the corner, a *literal* battle.

Back when I was studying, all high school students aged fourteen and above had to attend a compulsory Students' Summer Work Program.

It ran for six weeks during the eight-week school summer break, and its purpose was to instil a strong work ethic and cultural pride. It was also an opportunity for students to make friends with girls and guys from different schools and cities.

Overall, it was a well-intended program that encompassed social activities as well as physical labour in the form of picking up rubbish near roads and digging holes for plants. The plants helped to beautify Eritrea, as well as commemorate fallen soldiers who'd died for our freedom.

I had always been captivated by the summer program and couldn't wait for my turn to come around.

It finally did when I turned fourteen.

On the first day of the program, a line of about three hundred girls snaked around a field. This was the first year the females and males were separated, and I wasn't sure why. I didn't give much thought to it either because I was busy getting to know the other girls.

The beauty of these new acquaintances were their stories. Conversation seemed to fly this way and that, like a flock of wild birds in a glass dome.

My world seemed to come alive.

The air was sizzling.

I breathed in the energy, deeply and excitedly. It recharged my soul and invigorated my spirit.

After chatting and meeting new people, we had our names marked off a roll and were taken to big dorm halls where we'd be sleeping. The building was an old school, and it would be our home for the next six weeks.

The beds were mats on the floor, which was an immediate and stark reminder that the summer program was not about back support!

As I unpacked my bags, I started talking to Grace, a girl nearby with curly hair and lashes that practically combed the sky.

During the initial leisure time, Grace and I decided to walk around to explore the area. The grounds were expansive but sparse, with a grassy field outside the worn building. We weren't concentrating on the surroundings much, though; we were more engrossed in conversation.

So engrossed, in fact, that we completely lost track of time!

A student walked toward us and told us we'd missed our first meeting.

Oops!

'What was it about?' I asked.

'Mainly to nominate three leaders for three different groups of students. One girl was nominated for all three positions—Fiori Giovanni.'

'What? That's me!' I said. 'How? I wasn't even at the meeting?'

'You're Fiori?' she asked. 'Apparently there were other students from your school who knew about you, and nominated you. They said you ask a lot of questions and speak up for what's right.'

A tingling warmth spread through my body.

'Wow!' I said, standing just a bit taller than before.

The girl laughed. 'Don't get too excited. The teacher thought it was unfair that one person should have all the leadership positions, so one position went to another person.'

'Still, I'm thrilled.'

'One more thing,' the girl said. 'We also found out that the program is going to be different this year, due to the war.'

Ah yes, the war. The war between Eritrea and Ethiopia had become particularly intense in 1998, and things were getting worse in 1999—the year I was doing the summer program.

'How?' we asked.

'On top of the classes and manual work, we have to do military training.'

My smile slid away.

Grace turned to me, 'You know what this means, don't you? Training, training, training!'

Train, we did.

Rigorously.

An average day wasn't average at all, but overall, this is what it looked like.

We woke at 5:00 a.m. before the sun yawned into the sky.

We then dressed and walked to the field for marching or shooting lessons.

Marching might seem easy, but at that dream-dissolving hour, concentrating was a challenge. It was hard to know which leg was left or right, or whether we had legs at all!

We'd then have breakfast at 7:00 a.m.

Breakfast was a salt-less bread, which we gobbled hungrily. The absence of salt meant we didn't get thirsty easily.

At 8:00 a.m. we walked to designated locations for digging holes. This was usually thirty minutes to an hour away, or even more. The digging was back-breaking work because each hole had to be fifty centimetres wide by fifty centimetres deep, and we had to dig ten per day!

We'd finish at around 11:30 a.m., and walk back to the camp for lunch between 1:00 p.m. and 2:00 p.m.

Lunch (and dinner also) comprised of a lentil mixture eaten with the flat pancake bread called *injera*.

We were famished, and while I craved the rich, spiced curries from home, the blandness of camp food was to be expected.

We had rest and leisure between 2:00 p.m. and 4:00 p.m., but because I was the leader of two groups, I sometimes conducted activities such as drama plays and bonding exercises during these times. I usually perked up for these activities, but occasionally, admittedly, I was half asleep.

At 4:00 p.m., we'd walk to a different location to clean roads and pick up rubbish. Bending over constantly was tough, particularly after all the hole-digging from the morning.

After straightening our backs, we'd return to the camp by 6:00 p.m., ready to resume more military training of either shooting or marching.

Between 8:00 p.m. and 9:00 p.m. we'd wolf down dinner and then head straight to sleep, before getting up and doing it all again the next day.

Every day was certainly memorable, but I'll never forget the third day of camp in particular.

My body was throbbing and aching from all the digging and cleaning.

I limped over to the morning's military training, which unfortunately was learning to shoot and kill.

Suddenly, the aches and pains didn't matter because the mental fear of using a gun took over.

Many students stood with their heads held high, hoping to be shown how to use the firearms.

I didn't. I lurked at the back, huddling into myself, eyes low so that hopefully I wouldn't be chosen.

My tactic worked most of the time, but the downside of being well-known by others is that people seek you out.

On that third day, one of the soldiers found me at the back and said, 'Fiori, your turn!'

I dragged myself to the front.

The soldier handed me the rifle with a big smile. 'You can do it,' he encouraged.

I slowly and shakily took the gun, but practically dropped it immediately. It was heavier than I could've ever imagined. Or maybe it was the concrete-like fear in my fingertips that weighed it down. I was especially afraid that the gun would accidentally go off and kill everyone, including myself.

Seeing the terror in my eyes, the soldier calmly and slowly gave me instructions. Once he was done, he said, 'Now, just shoot. It's easy. You can do it.'

Just shoot.

Sounded so easy.

I exhaled slowly, closed my eyes and started to press down on the cold trigger.

I stopped.

I saw flashes of dead bodies before my eyes, bodies I had seen over the course of my life.

I couldn't bear the thought of pulling the trigger. I wanted no part of the machines that caused such gruesome injuries and deaths.

I lowered the gun.

The soldier got up close and whispered, 'Fiori, you're one of the smartest girls here. You're a natural leader and everyone is watching you. You need to be a positive role model for these girls. You aren't just responsible for yourself; you're responsible for all these females, and your country.'

Gosh, no pressure!

I sighed, got into position, and put my finger on the trigger again.

I pressed a tiny bit, then just a little bit more.

I squeezed my eyes shut, hard, as though that would block out the sound of the upcoming bang.

More images flashed before my eyes.

A head blown off here.

A woman sliced there.

A gnarled corpse.

A tapestry of guts.

A pile of limbs.

Death.

Suffering.

Blood.

Pain.

I shook my head, stood up straight and said, 'I can't. I just can't.'

Everyone went quiet.

No one had refused a soldier's order.

All the girls seemed to be holding their breath.

'Fine,' he said, his tone changing from caring to cutting. 'If you don't shoot, I'll shoot *you*. Don't think I won't, because I've killed many.'

We both knew it was a threat, but that didn't stop me from trembling, and from making another attempt at shooting the gun.

I got into position again, but the trembling was so bad I could barely hold the gun still. It was swaying from side to side.

The soldier started clearing his throat nervously.

He started shuffling from side to side.

Eventually, worried for everyone's safety, including his own, he grabbed the gun from me.

The breath I'd been holding gushed out, taking every ounce of nervous energy with it. I wanted to melt into the grass from exhaustion and relief.

'Don't get too comfortable, Fiori,' he snapped. 'There are consequences for not following orders or not completing tasks successfully.'

The soldier dished out my punishment.

I had to hold a large, heavy rock (of course) while walking across the length of the field, *on my knees.*

As I knelt down and held the rock, memories of all my school punishments came flooding back.

But this punishment was far more excruciating than anything I'd ever experienced. At school I knelt in one spot. Here, I had to lug my weight from one knee to the other, over a rough and ragged surface.

Within minutes my skin was scraped and bleeding, leaving a trail of blood.

I felt as though I was dragging myself over a field of broken glass. The sharpness stabbed and slashed at my knees, while my shoulders and arms screamed from having to hold the cumbersome rock.

But, I never once wished I'd shot the gun. Better that there was blood on my knees than blood on my hands. I couldn't live with myself if I accidentally shot someone, much less intentionally did so, as they intended to train me. I'd rather crawl to the ends of the earth on my knees than kill or injure someone while standing.

The soldier basked in the groans of my agony.

He didn't realise that I was in a position of strength.

I was in control.

I was creating a map of resilience.

Every scratch and scar on my skin would serve as lifelong arrows, pointing me in the right direction during times of struggle.

When I eventually finished my punishment, with everyone watching me, he smiled smugly.

On the inside, I smiled too.

He assumed I felt humiliated.

He was wrong.

I felt triumphant.

I had completed the punishment.

I hobbled away with my map.

Over the next two weeks my knees eventually healed. Just as well too, because there was another gun-related surprise in store.

One night we were awakened at 1:00 a.m. by the shrill sound of a soldier's whistle.

The whistle indicated we'd be having military training exercises in the dark.

At that hour, the whistle was like a whip, lashing my dreams in two.

My eyes would fling open.

My heart would pin-ball around my ribcage.

There was no time to absorb the shock, though. I, along with all the others, would immediately have to get dressed and line up outside the dorm room to receive orders.

On previous nights, we'd been taken on walking drills that lasted eight hours, sixteen hours, and once, even twenty-four hours! During those drills, my heels would crack and my toes would bleed.

This time, it wasn't a walking drill.

We were made to walk, but to a completely unfamiliar place. When we arrived at our destination, the commander stopped and said, 'We are now close to the Ethiopian border where the Eritrean and Ethiopian soldiers are fighting.'

Gulp.

What?

'As we walk along,' he continued, 'if you hear the enemy Ethiopian soldiers start firing, drop to the ground. Don't make a sound, even if you're shot at.'

Shot at?

SHOT AT?!

We all looked at each other.

Beads of sweat exploded on my hairline.

I didn't want to keep walking, but had to.

With the moonlight's haze glowing brightly above us, I felt exposed and vulnerable.

We all moved together, tightly, in a pack.

I could feel the quickening of other students' breath on my neck.

I could hear a stifled cry, a swallowed sob.

And then it came.

A shot!

We ducked.

We dropped.

We screamed.

Be silent? Not possible!

The gunshot sent adrenalin firing through our bodies as we fearfully waited for an excruciating pierce in some part of our body.

Amidst the earthquake of gasping, we realised no one had been hurt.

No one had been shot.

Relief!

After a few minutes, we slowly stood, bodies low, ready to crouch again in an instant.

We thought we were safe for the moment.

We forgot about the commander!

He angrily marched over.

He spoke in a low hiss. 'We fired a test shot. We fired it to see whether you would follow instructions and not scream. You failed!'

With that, he went to a nearby tree and broke off a thin stick.

We all took a nervous step back.

We knew what was coming.

He walked down the line, lashing at us.

If you were hit, you had to swallow the scream. You couldn't make a noise.

For once, I didn't get any of the punishment because his swiping was random.

When the commander finished his outburst, he issued his instruction again: 'Next time you hear a shot, lie on the ground *without making a sound.*'

He then returned to the bushes.

Although we were all rattled, and many were bruised, there was a sense of relief that the test shots had come from the commander, not from the Ethiopian army. But, who's to say the next round of bullets *wouldn't* be from the enemy? They'd heard gunfire now.

As those thoughts filled my brain, the next shot was fired.

We collectively crumpled.

Most of our noises were softer now.

But one girl screamed! This was followed by all of us making a *shhhhh* sound to try to keep her quiet.

It was too late.

There he was, the commander, in front of us, angry as hell.

He shone a torch into our group.

We were still hunched over; we had to protect our eyes from the light.

'You!' he yelled to the girl who had tears streaming down her face. 'Come!'

He grabbed the girl by the shoulder and spun her to face us.

He handed the torch to a student, who shone the light onto both of them.

We had no idea what sort of punishment she'd get.

She cried uncontrollably now.

But rather than hurt her, the commander simply issued a dark warning. 'Don't let fear control you. If one of you cries, all of you could die.'

His words hung in the air like toxic particles.

Many of these students had *wanted* to fight for their country, but now, war felt frighteningly real.

The commander directed the crying girl back into the group.

During the next round of shots, everyone was quiet.

In fact, we were quiet for the rest of the night, even as we walked to the next training location.

At this new location, which seemed much further from the border, we were taken to the top of a mountain.

We were told that during war, enemies are everywhere: at the top of mountains, at the bottom of mountains, behind bushes, and inside our heads. While the commander couldn't run training drills inside our heads, he could definitely run them on top of mountains.

And there she was, in front of us. The moonlight coated her rugged ridges. If not for the training, I would have taken a moment to soak in her beauty.

For the first drill, a small group of us climbed up the mountain and were shown how to shoot the enemy from the peak.

Some of the girls eagerly volunteered for this activity because it involved gun skills.

Not me, of course.

I prayed that the soldier wouldn't call me up.

My prayers were answered.

I wasn't called.

I looked up at the night sky and thanked God.

I also prayed that my shoulder blades would sprout mighty wings, allowing me to fly to the heavens, away from guns and violence and war.

But, I flew nowhere that night.

I simply walked back down the mountain, wishing the military training and summer camp would end.

And thankfully, eventually, it did.

Once summer camp was over I returned to school in Keren, but things were different now.

There was uneasiness in the air.

It oozed thickly around me, around everyone.

In May of 2000, within a few months of the camp finishing, the uneasiness turned into outright fear. The war between Eritrea and Ethiopia was raging all day and all night.

The Ethiopian soldiers who had previously fought only on the borders had invaded Eritrea and taken over many cities.

Eritrean blood flowed thick and fast.

There was torture and rape; there were executions and prison roundups.

Many Eritreans fled from city to city to stay alive.

Not surprisingly, the country was in chaos.

Most schools were shut down.

Students stopped studying and started fighting on the frontline. They wanted to make a difference.

I too wanted to make a difference, but couldn't and wouldn't do it by killing. I wanted to save the world with peace, debate, negotiation, and compromise. That's why I kept showing up at school each morning—I kept looking for my purpose.

Thankfully, my school was still open, but each day there were less students and less teachers.

I was expecting bad news to come.

It did.

One morning a woman told us there'd be no more classes. She explained that many students and teachers had chosen to fight, and she outlined our options. We could either fight, or help the war effort in other ways.

One of the ways she outlined caught my attention.

She explained that the government was in desperate need of people with first aid training to assist in the military hospital.

I had first aid training.

That's how I would help!

I sighed with relief. Finally, my sense of helplessness was replaced with a sense of purpose.

That purpose helped me get out of bed the next day, when I could easily have stayed hidden under the covers, afraid of what I'd see at the hospital.

I was right to be afraid.

The minute I walked through the doors, I wanted to run.

Run away from the cries and the moans.

The smell of vomit, of urine.

The smell of sickness and death.

But I remembered my purpose.

I kept walking, deep into the hospital.

As I walked, my mouth felt dry.

My legs began to shake.

Nausea washed over me, and my head spun.

To be honest, my reaction surprised me.

I had already witnessed brutality, atrocities, injuries, and death in my life. I had seen blood and murder. I thought I'd be prepared. But there was no preparation for *this*. It was like a scene from a gruesome horror movie.

The injuries were stomach-churning.

Exploded organs.

Scattered guts.

Limbs missing.

And blood, *so* much blood.

When I finally steadied myself, I stood as tall as I could, and kept moving.

When soldiers saw me close by, they begged for pain relief or food or death. Anything to ease the suffering.

Some of their screams were blood curdling. Many times I had to fight back tears.

I reported to my supervisor as quickly as I could. I took a deep, vomit-suppressing breath and told her I was ready to begin my duties. But the minute she saw my ghostly face, she said, 'I think the kitchen will be better for you. They need a lot of help in there.'

I could have hugged her, but I sped to the kitchen before she could change her mind!

The kitchen was a room filled with steam, chopping and organised chatter.

I jumped right in. This, I was capable of doing.

I cut, diced, mixed, stirred, mopped, and cleaned—all proudly.

In my own mind, I saw the other students and myself as soldiers. Young Eritrean citizens doing our part for our country. We may not have been fighting on the frontline, but we were battling nonetheless. Battling the enemy by saving lives and feeding our fighters.

Every day, I got out of bed to do battle.

The hospital was the war zone.

It was exhausting, but at least I was able to go home each night.

In some ways, though, there was no reprieve. Once home, I could see the wounds and couldn't eat. I could hear the cries and couldn't sleep.

It was a constant battle in my mind.

Along with everyone else, I soldiered on, day in and day out.

No two days were the same.

But one day, something was *quite* different.

I walked through one of the wards to get to the kitchen, and I noticed a young boy lying in a corner. There were never enough beds to keep up with the casualties, so soldiers lay wherever there was a spare inch of floor.

When I looked closer, it was Ermias, a close friend from school.

One of his arms had been blown off, and bits of flesh hung from his mangled stump.

I raced over.

I fetched towels and bandages.

I stopped the bleeding as best I could, biting my lip as retches thumped their way up my throat.

I remembered Ermias well from school. He had two dimples that skipped along his face all day. Nothing ever seemed to bother him in class. Yet, here he was, a butchered version of his former self.

He opened his eyes slightly.

'Ermias, it's Fiori from school,' I said. 'You're not alone. I'm here.'

He looked at me for at least a minute before tears slid from the sides of both his eyes. I tended to him as much as I could, but had to get back to the kitchen. I called a nurse and asked that she please help him.

For the rest of the day, I visited Ermias every spare moment I could. I fed him lentils, stroked his forehead, and cried into his hair.

Ermias was my friend. The war had done this to him.

After a few days, he miraculously started gaining some strength, and began speaking.

'Fiori, thank you for looking after me.'

I burst into tears looking at his stump. 'I couldn't help with your injury though.'

'It was just an arm,' he said. 'It's one less thing to carry.'

I laughed amidst my crying. The cheeky Ermias was making a comeback.

When I saw him the next day, it was obvious he been operated on overnight. He was connected to a drip, had fresh bandages, and was lying on a bed.

'How are you feeling?' I asked.

'I'm in constant, aching pain,' he whispered. 'So, pretty good.'

'Don't joke, Ermias. How much pain are you in?'

'A lot. I feel like there's a knife constantly stabbing into my stump.'

I shuddered at the thought, and immediately sought out a doctor to provide more medication.

On a selfish level, I loved having Ermias at the hospital. I looked forward to seeing him, and I often arrived earlier than my shift to have a chat with him.

One morning, though, he wasn't in his bed.

'Are you looking for the one-armed boy?' asked a nurse.

'Ermias. Yes, where is he?'

'Back on the frontline.'

'But, his arm!' I yelped. 'He was in so much pain. He'd barely healed.'

She shrugged. 'He wanted to go. He felt strong enough.'

I felt as though the biggest, darkest cloud descended upon me. I imagined Ermias on the frontline with only one arm. How would he cope?

The answer is: he wouldn't.

Sure enough, he returned two months later.

This time he had one leg missing.

As soon as that injury 'healed,' he chose to fight again.

I wasn't expecting him to return.

He didn't.

He was one of many friends killed in the war.

Sadly, Eritrean soldiers were dropping like flies: men, women, children—all fighting and dying. Even the elderly gave their precious remaining years to fight the enemy.

Ethiopia had a massive population compared to Eritrea. They had the luxury of recruiting fit, young men. Eritrea didn't have that luxury, which is why *everyone* was invited to defend the country.

It's possible I would be invited to fight too, very soon.

But like my Uncle Debesay, I didn't see war as a path to greatness or peace.

If I wanted to avoid becoming another dead soldier, I would need to take a risk.

I would need to take action.

I would need to escape Eritrea.

CHAPTER THREE

LOVING AND LEAVING

Even if you sit in the wreckage of an attempt, you defy your destiny through the courage of your intent.

Once I'd made the decision to escape Eritrea, I no longer saw my world through the bloodied lens of suffering and war.

I no longer lowered my head to avoid seeing death; I raised it to the sky, to see signs of life.

As I looked up, the sky showed me my limits, of which there were none.

Soon, I would fly like the birds.

Soon, I would enjoy freedom.

But first, I had to share the plans of my escape with Mum.

I made the trip from Keren to Asmara, where my parents were living now.

Normally, I'd have to tell Dad first, but devastatingly, he was then in prison nearby on suspicion of working with the Ethiopians, the enemy. The suspicion arose for the strangest reason too. When my dad found out that Maidamu (his birth city) had been invaded by Ethiopian soldiers, he immediately travelled to Maidamu from Asmara to help his elderly grandmothers, who couldn't flee. He knew he might be killed by Ethiopian soldiers, but he was willing to die protecting his family.

When he got to Maidamu, Ethiopian soldiers were scattered throughout the city, and while they *did* in fact threaten to kill Dad, they were more focused on destroying, raping, and pillaging. They moved on from Maidamu after a few days, leaving death, destruction, and desecration in their wake.

Once the Eritrean soldiers eventually got to Maidamu to protect its citizens, they asked Dad why he'd returned there when nearly everyone else had fled. Dad explained that he wanted to protect his elderly grandmothers who didn't have the strength to run.

They didn't believe him. They thought he was working with the Ethiopians. As a result, he was locked up.

The thought of my dad being in prison was horrifying.

How was he being treated?

Was he getting enough food?

Was he being tortured?

It was impossible to know when he'd return, if ever.

Although I couldn't tell Dad of my escape plans, I knew he would be proud of my decision. After all, he ran *into* danger to protect the ones he loved, so he'd support me running *away* from danger, if it kept me alive.

Knowing I had his silent blessing gave me strength.

Strength to tell Mum.

I picked my moment carefully one night when Mum was relaxed but also distracted.

I sat opposite her in the lounge room as she folded some washed clothes.

My mouth felt like sand.

My palms felt like the sea.

I had an ocean of uncertainty in front of me.

I decided it was best to just launch into the full story, just to tell Mum the whole thing without taking a breath or waiting for her initial reaction.

'Mum, I'm thinking of leaving Eritrea,' I said. 'As you know, the government won't give me permission to leave, so I'm going to travel to Tesenai by bus, stay at a hotel there, and try to find a guide to secretly take me into Sudan. Tesenai is close to the Sudan border, so it shouldn't be too hard to find someone. I know it's dangerous to leave, but it's also dangerous to stay. When the time is right, I would like to help Amanuel leave Eritrea too.'

I stopped talking.

I took a breath.

I waited.

Mum put down the shirts she was folding.

She just stared at me.

And stared some more, for what seemed like an eternity.

Eventually, she got up from the couch.

I got up too, though I wasn't sure what was going to happen.

She walked over and stood in front of me.

She gave me the tightest hug ever.

I closed my eyes and enjoyed its warmth and surrendered to its power. It was the kind of hug a mother gives her child when saying goodbye. The kind of hug that is so bitter and sorrowful that you don't want to accept it, yet never want it to end.

We sat for hours, not saying a word.

I cried.

Mum cried.

Our tears did all the talking.

At a moment like this, most mothers would start giving their fifteen-year-old daughter advice and warnings.

My mother didn't.

She knew I'd lived a full, independent life filled with twists and turns that forced me to become mature, fast.

She knew I'd have done copious amounts of research.

She knew I'd have weighed the decision on a million different scales.

She knew I could die.

Most of all, she knew she might never see me again, but that escaping Eritrea would provide the best chance of survival, and of working toward a better future.

When she eventually spoke, Mum simply asked, 'How can I help?'

Being a typical teenager, I replied, 'I've got this. I just need money.'

Mum smiled.

'Also I need a big favour,' I continued. 'Please tell Amanuel of my decision once I'm gone. If I tell him, I'm not sure what he'll do, and I'm not sure what *I'll* do. It will be too painful for both of us. And it's safer as well. If he tells a friend, and that friend tells a government official, the risk of getting caught is great.'

Mum nodded. 'I'll tell him. And yes, I'll give you some money. But first, promise to call me the moment you land anywhere, and at all times, whenever possible.'

'I promise.'

'I'll pray for you, Fiori, every moment of every day,' Mum said. 'You'll need my prayers more than you'll ever know.'

<hr />

Within a few days, my plan was in motion.

And Mum was right, I definitely needed her prayers, because I was escaping.

Really escaping.

I sat on an old bus headed to Tesenai, the Eritrean city that bordered Sudan.

This bus would take me to a new life.

A life of *my* choosing.

As the bus chugged forward, it left behind a deep cough of smoke.

I, on the other hand, left behind a dark cloud of secrets.

Apart from Mum, no one knew where I was, or what I was doing. Fleeing my country was illegal, and the potential repercussions were severe.

Sweat oozed through my palms, but I tried to remain cool.

The bus journey would be twelve long hours, but thankfully the driver informed us he'd stop regularly for breaks where we could stretch our legs and get some fresh air.

When the first break came around, I stepped into the sunlight and stretched out my back.

I looked to the right of me, and I saw someone, a lady from my village. 'Amleset, is that you?' I asked.

'Hello Fiori,' she said, smiling. But she quickly sized up the fact that I, at such a young age, was on a bus to Tesenai, alone, and made the correct assumption that I was escaping. (Otherwise, why was I going to such a faraway Eritrean border city?)

Her expression changed. She walked up and gave me a long, reassuring hug. She then made small talk, and when it was time to get back on the bus, squeezed my hand and said, 'Keep safe.'

While that was the plan, things didn't quite go as planned.

After nearly twelve hours, it was at the last checkpoint that I ran into trouble.

'Papers,' ordered a checkpoint soldier.

I handed over my student card, which was a legal identification card that allowed me to travel from city to city. The student card got me through all the checkpoints up until now, but because Tesenai was a border city that many young people used as a springboard to Sudan, the soldier was suspicious.

'Why are you travelling to Tesenai?' he asked.

'I'm ... I'm visiting my aunt.'

He flicked the student card back at me. 'I don't believe you. Get your bag. You're coming with me.'

The lady from my village, Amleset, came over. 'Why are you taking her? She hasn't done anything wrong.'

The soldier's eyebrows raised like fighting cats. 'What did you say?'

The power of his voice practically blew Amleset back to her seat.

'What have I done wrong?' I asked. 'Where are you taking me?'

His eyes drilled into mine. 'Wherever I choose. Get your things.'

The soldier ordered two teenage boys off the bus as well.

I exchanged fearful looks with both of them.

Once off the bus, the soldier separated me from the boys, sending them with a different soldier.

This was not a good start to my new life!

It was dusk, and the soldier ordered me to walk with him toward the city of Tesenai, the very city to which I was trying to get.

We walked for about twenty minutes before reaching a building.

It was a jail.

Oh no!

My steps became heavier and slower.

The soldier grabbed my arm and pulled me forward. 'That's right. Keep moving.'

'But ... but, I was just visiting my aunt, I promise!'

He pulled me again, all the way into the building.

The prison had a dismal and dangerous feel to it.

Perspiration tumbled over my brows as I took in the awful surroundings. The walls were discoloured and cracked. It smelt like a pile of compost.

I was taken around a corner.

In front of me was a cell with a handful of women who appeared to be in their twenties and thirties. Initially their expressions were vacant and distant, but the minute they saw me, they squared their shoulders and moved toward the bars.

One smiled ominously.

One gave me a filthy look.

One opened her legs and smiled.

I looked at the soldier and pleaded, 'I was just visiting family. Please don't lock me up.'

He just grabbed my arm, took me to the cell, opened it, and flung me inside.

Fear thumped through every square inch of my body. It drained my lungs of breath. It turned my legs to butter.

I felt like a mouse thrown into a pit of hungry, hissing snakes.

The women instantly coiled around me.

A guard yelled at them.

They slunk away.

With my back to the bars, my shaking legs gave way, and I sat on the floor. My small, cloth bag was slung diagonally around the front of my body, and I clutched it tightly.

One woman walked over, swinging her hips and smiling like a she-devil.

She had a scar that branded her forehead and twisted down her left cheek.

I tried to stop my knees from rattling, but I just couldn't.

She bent down and stroked my face and shoulder.

She smelt like a rotting carcass.

I desperately wanted to cover my nose, but couldn't, in case it offended her.

My body shuddered more and more.

'I'm going to fuck you,' she hissed.

I looked away, partly out of fear, partly out of revulsion. Her vile breath was practically burning my skin.

'You want to kiss me?' she invited.

The thought of her lips on mine, her tongue slithering into my mouth, made me want to vomit.

I gagged.

'Kill her!' one woman called out. 'Kill the bitch!'

The others started pacing and glaring.

Another whispered, *'Kill, kill, kill.'*

My heart was thumping in my ears. I closed my eyes and savoured the sound of my heartbeat, because I wasn't sure if I'd ever hear it again.

I thought of Dad. Was this his life too? Was he cowering in a jail cell, wondering if each moment would be his last?

Just when I thought all hope was lost, the scar-faced woman who had been sitting in front of me spun around, snarling at the other women. 'Shut up you whores! She's mine!'

The women recoiled, protecting their heads as though she was going to hit them. They moved to the edges of the cell where they lurked and stared.

Scar-lady turned back to me, squeezing my face with one hand, whispering, 'They're going to kill you tonight. You have to get out of here. I can help you escape. Do you want my help?'

I blinked what must have been dozens of times. I opened my mouth to speak, but nothing came out. How did I talk to someone who no doubt was capable of killing me too, but yet, may somehow help me escape?

Seeing my mix of confusion and hope, she burst into laughter, revelling in my gullibility.

The other women joined in the laughter.

Some giggled.

Most guffawed.

Scar-lady asked, 'Are you good at sex?'

'She's too sweet,' a different inmate said.

'Let's fuck her brains out,' someone shrieked.

Scar-lady tried to pull at my top.

I couldn't stay still and defenceless anymore.

I screamed and pushed her away. I wouldn't go down without a fight.

Hearing my scream, a guard walked up to the bars.

Then, the strangest thing happened.

The women, including scar-lady, instantly turned their attention to the guard.

It's as though I didn't exist anymore.

They dove against the cell's rails, banging the bars and yelling out filthy propositions.

'I'll suck you off!'

'I'm wet!'

'Come in and fuck me!'

The guard rolled his eyes and just banged his stick against the rails. 'If you want your food, settle down!'

There was immediate quiet.

He unlocked a covered gap in the bars to pass through a small pot of lentil water and some bread. The women grabbed it desperately, with scar-lady taking her share first.

I was hungry but didn't dare move.

I was just relieved the women were preoccupied.

Thankfully, that preoccupation turned into post-dinner tiredness.

Oddly, they seemed content for a while.

I stayed in my little spot and decided to bunker down for the night.

Scar-lady sprawled herself in front of me. I wasn't sure if that was to protect me or pounce on me.

Amazingly, she fell asleep instantly and barely moved the whole night.

Other women stared and mouthed words at me, but none dared inch closer.

I tried to stay awake as much as possible, but my eyelids constantly collapsed under an avalanche of worry and exhaustion.

When I awoke the next morning, I was in one piece, lying along the filthy ground.

My attempts to stay awake had failed, but fortunately my goal to stay alive had been successful.

I pulled myself into a seated position and rubbed my eyes.

Scar-face was having a heated conversation with someone nearby, which probably was what woke me in the first place.

As my brain slowly kicked into gear, a guard walked toward the cell.

The women who were awake jumped up and started harassing him. They were less boisterous than the night before, but eager nonetheless.

The guard pointed at me and said, 'You, come.'

What did that mean? Was I being released?

He opened the cell and took me to a small room where a soldier was seated and waiting. The soldier motioned for me to sit, which I did, quietly and obediently.

'Where are you from? Where have you lived?' he asked.

'My family is in Asmara,' I replied. 'I have lived in several places over the years, including most recently, Keren.'

His voice became like a wielded sword: 'Keren, the city of sluts! Keren, the city where every girl asks you to fuck them!'

I clenched my fists.

I had obediently sat down.

I had obediently answered his question.

I would have obediently answered *all* his questions, but after the night I had, I wasn't obediently going to be insulted. Every sizzling nerve-ending in my body was like the wick of a firecracker, which he lit with his unfair words.

'Yes, I have lived in Keren,' I snapped, looking him up and down. 'But no, I would never ask *you* to touch me.'

The soldier sat back in his chair, his face nearly exploding. 'What did you say, you little whore?! You're going to regret the day you opened your mouth. You're lucky I don't kill you with my bare hands!'

I backed away from him, not expecting such an aggressive, physical threat.

Just as I did, an administrative clerk entered our room. I thought he was coming in to calm the situation, but he simply wanted to pass on a private message.

The soldier pushed himself up from his chair, glaring at me. 'This isn't over. Get out of my sight!'

I swallowed hard to lubricate my throat.

The guard took me back to my cell.

While I was relieved to get away from the soldier, I was devastated to be returning to the cage.

The women were thrilled to have me back though. I was their little plaything.

Why couldn't I have ignored the soldier's insults?

Curiously, I was only back in the cell for a few moments when another guard came to get me out again.

The women voiced their displeasure.

Inwardly, I did too.

Was this some type of torture? Or did the clerk's message have something to do with me being removed again? I think it did, because as I was led out of the cell I heard two women speaking. One of the voices sounded familiar. Who was it?

When I turned the corner, I saw Amleset, the woman from the bus journey. I wanted to jump for joy at the sight of her!

The guard gave us space to talk, but lurked nearby.

'I came as soon as I could,' Amleset said, hugging me. She then turned to the nearby lady. 'This is Rahel. She's well connected and has negotiated your release.'

My release?!

I really *did* want to jump for joy now.

Rahel was a tall, meticulously-groomed, heavily-perfumed woman with lips so glossy I could nearly see my reflection in them. She shook my hand briefly and firmly.

'Thank you for helping me,' I said, realising I'd have to be formal with her.

As suspected, Rahel had no time for niceties. She got down to business, advising me of how much bribe money she'd need to get me out of jail. She also told me, in hushed tones, that she knew people who could secretly take me into Sudan, but I would need to pay her a certain amount for that too.

The figure was exorbitant, nearly all the money I had. But the pain of being ripped off by Rahel was nothing compared to the potential pain of being ripped apart by the women. And the former meant freedom.

'I have the money,' I said, pulling it from my cloth bag and handing it to her.

Rahel nodded, walked into the hallway, and communicated something to the guard in sign language. She slipped him some money and said to us, 'It's done. Let's get out of this hole.'

I couldn't believe how quickly and easily I was released when bribe money and someone with influence were involved. I thought of Dad, and hoped one day he could walk out of jail too.

For me, prison had been a scary, surreal experience, and one I never wanted to re-live again.

'You're safe now,' Amleset reassured.

'Thank you so much to both of you,' I said. 'What will happen now?'

'Rahel owns a hotel and bar,' Amleset explained. 'I will stay at the hotel overnight, and head back to Asmara first thing tomorrow. I'll pass on a message to your mum as soon as I get back that you're safe and well.'

'Yes, please do that. She'll be worried, and she made me promise to keep in touch. Also, can you please pass on another message?'

'Of course.'

'Just before leaving, Mum told me she'd try to track down some distant relatives in Sudan, to ask if I can stay with them. The plan is that when I get to Sudan, I'll ask the guide to call Mum for the address details, and then ask the guide to take me to those relatives. Please tell Mum that I'm sticking to the plan, but that I'm not sure exactly when I'll be in Sudan.'

'I will,' Amleset promised. 'For now you will lay low in Rahel's home, which is in the same compound as her hotel and bar. She'll hire a guide who will eventually smuggle you over the border and take you to the nearest Sudanese town, Kassala. You're in safe hands.'

Amleset kept saying I was in safe hands with Rahel, but my gut told me otherwise.

Rahel had certainly helped me, but I had paid handsomely and astronomically for her services. It was a lucrative cash transaction for her, not a selfless act of kindness. And anyway, I was not sure there was much kindness in her.

Still, I had limited options.

We all took a taxi to the compound, and once there, Amleset bid me farewell because her hotel room was in a separate part of the large compound. She told me she would be running errands in Tesenai during the day, sleeping at the hotel at night, and leaving early for Asmara the next morning.

I wouldn't see her again, which made me sad. It was solely because of her that I was out of jail. I hugged her long and hard, sharing words of thanks as I did.

'You will be safe now,' she reassured. She then released herself from my hug and walked away, leaving me with Rahel.

At Rahel's home, I immediately asked to use the bathroom. I had crossed my legs for so long in prison, I felt my bladder would explode.

When I came out, I saw that Rahel had heated up an aromatic Eritrean curry for me, which she served with piles of *injera*.

'Eat, you must be hungry.'

I wasn't hungry; I was *famished*.

I thanked Rahel while tearing off *injera* and wrapping it around thick chunks of beef and vegetables, chewing each mouthful fast and furiously.

'Keep eating,' she said. 'I need to go out but will be back soon.'

Within ten minutes Rahel returned with good news: 'I've found you a guide. Be prepared. He could come on any night of the week, depending on the safety of the route. In the meantime, stay here in my home and wait. And don't talk to anyone.'

I finished my mouthful. 'Thank you, yes, I understand. Will I stay in one of your hotel rooms?'

'You'll stay in my bedroom,' she said. 'I'll treat you like my daughter. Once you've finished eating, go and have a bath and a nap. It's the first room on the right. If you need anything at all, let me know.'

'Thank you again so much,' I said.

I was grateful—I really was. But my gratefulness was tempered with suspicion. Rahel was a deal maker, a tough businesswoman. Her attempts at being maternal were solid but not sincere.

After I'd finished eating I walked to her bedroom, which was lavishly decorated, just like she was. The air inside was plump with the scent of her perfume. The room was like a palace compared to the prison.

In fact, I was dying to wash the prison smell off me, so I ran a hot bath and poured some oils into it. I then removed my clothes and sunk into the steaming water.

'Ahhhhh,' I said.

I just lay there, still.

Hugged by the water.

Embraced by the oils.

I could feel the dirt dissolve away.

But I could only relax for a moment.

The sweet smell of Rahel's perfumes reminded me to always stay alert.

I washed myself with soap, and after drying off, I put on a fresh set of clothes from my small bag.

Although I wanted to stay watchful, I could barely keep my eyes open. Rahel had earlier suggested I take a nap, and I realised it was a good idea.

I literally stumbled into her soft bed where I instantly slept.

I only awoke because of chatter and laughter from her bar. The bar was in another part of the compound, but the noise carried.

I blinked with crumply eyes to check the time.

It was 3:00 p.m. I had slept solidly for hours!

I was still in one piece too, which was a good sign.

In fact, I saw that Rahel had left a platter of food on the dressing table for me while I was asleep.

Maybe my reservations about her were premature?

Hungry again, I feasted on the fruit, washing it down with a jug of orange juice.

With a belly full of food and feeling rested, I walked to the kitchen where Rahel was busily doing paperwork.

'Did you sleep well?' she asked while scribbling on some documents.

'I did. Thank you for your hospitality, your bedroom, the food, everything. I appreciate it all. Is there anything I can help you with?'

She smiled and looked up, 'I would love some coffee.'

'Certainly, I can make coffee.'

Making a cup of coffee in Eritrea isn't just about making a cup of coffee—it's an actual ceremony. The ceremony takes anywhere from an hour to two hours, and its purpose is to bring friends and family together.

Rahel wasn't my friend, but making her coffee was a way to show my gratefulness.

I lit some incense to signify the ceremony was beginning.

CHAPTER THREE

I was relieved when Rahel didn't stop her work to try to chat with me. I felt more relaxed not having to talk, and not being watched.

I poured green beans into a pot and started roasting them over a gas burner.

The scent reminded me of when Mum and other women in our village made coffee. I reminisced for a moment. I remembered how the vines of steam from the roasting beans and the tendrils of smoke from the incense would curl around passing people, pulling them in, entwining them together in joy, laughter, and conversation. They were beautiful times.

But, it was back to the present.

I shook the beans around the pan. They transformed from green to brown, like spring strolling into autumn.

Just as the oil appeared on the beans, I removed the pan from the heat and presented it to Rahel, who stopped work to momentarily breathe in the roasted scent.

She smiled before returning to her papers.

If there were more people in the room, I would have walked around to each, allowing the delicious steam to waft toward them.

I poured the medium-roasted beans onto a round, woven mat.

Once the beans cooled, I ground them with a mortar and pestle.

'Smells like a nice roast,' Rahel said while punching numbers into a calculator.

'Thank you. I hope it tastes good.'

At this point, I added a small amount of water into a *jebena*, which is an earthenware pot with a long neck and a thin spout coming from that neck. I spooned the ground beans into the top of the long neck.

I then placed it back onto the gas burner.

As the coffee began bubbling out of the top, I took the *jebena* off the burner, pouring some of the coffee from within it into a cup.

I then re-poured that same coffee into the top of the *jebena* and placed it back onto the burner to continue percolating.

I did this around five times until the coffee looked and smelt ready.

I then placed the *jebena* in a woven holder, a kind of small, handle-less basket. I tilted it slightly so the beans would settle to the bottom rather than float around in the coffee liquid.

That settling process was going to take around six minutes, so in the meantime I grabbed a corn cob and made popcorn over the gas burner. Popcorn is a traditional snack to enjoy with Eritrean coffee, and I knew Rahel would want the ceremony to be proper and complete.

Once the beans had settled, I poured the coffee from the *jebena* into a small, wide-rimmed cup without a handle, known as a *finjal*.

I passed it to Rahel. 'It's ready.'

She smiled, took the cup, and sipped the hot coffee slowly. 'Good. Very good. I can see you've done this a few times before.'

'Yes, with my mum and relatives. I'm glad you like it.'

As she drank her coffee, she asked if I could help her prepare food for dinner as well.

I happily agreed.

I milled around the kitchen, working hard.

By early evening, though, my eyelids felt heavy. 'I've finished, Rahel. I might go to bed now; I'm quite tired.'

She nodded. 'Thank you for your help, and sleep well. I'm going to work at my bar now, but I may need to get items from my bedroom tonight, so don't lock the door. If I need to enter, I'll be quiet and won't disturb you.'

'Sure, I'll keep the door unlocked.'

I walked to her room, and after brushing my teeth, I crawled under the bed covers and immediately swam madly and deeply into an ocean of dreams. Whales were chasing me. Sharks were circling me.

'Wake up.'

Amanuel was in my dream. He was telling me to wake up.

'I can't, Amanuel,' I said in my dream. 'I'm soooo tired. I just need to sleep.'

'WAKE UP!'

I sat bolt upright in Rahel's bed.

It wasn't a dream at all.

There was a middle-aged man standing over me. He was reeking of alcohol, swaying on the spot. 'Are you ... are you the virgin? I paid more for you ... for the virgin.'

I jumped out of the bed and pushed past him.

'Who are you?' I demanded.

He couldn't answer. He just stumbled out of the room.

I slammed the door behind him.

I sat on the bed, clutching my chest, trying to slow my pounding heart.

Within moments another drunk man barged through the door.

I leapt up, lunged at him, kicked him in the shin, and pushed him out, this time locking the door.

He banged his fists against the door. 'You the girl from the nuns' camp? I paid my money, you bitch!'

'That girl doesn't work here!' I said. 'Go away!'

The man began shouting. 'I paid Rahel just five minutes ago! You're a fucked-up bitch! I'm gonna talk to her right now!'

'Good!' I yelled. 'Do it!'

My instinct about Rahel was correct. She was prostituting me out, probably charging double or triple because I was a virgin.

Within minutes, someone else tried to turn the doorknob.

'Go away!' I screamed.

'Fiori, it's Rahel! Open this door now! I told you not to lock it!'

I opened the door.

'Why is this door locked?!' she yelled.

'Because you're sending men to my room for sex!'

'How dare you accuse me of such a thing, Fiori!' she snapped, pretending to be outraged at such a suggestion. 'I am too angry to talk to you right now. Keep this door *open* or I'll throw you onto the street!'

She then stormed away.

My whole body trembled.

I closed the door with shaking hands, and slumped against it.

I hugged my knees, just like I did in prison.

I huffed and puffed with breathless anger and fear.

I wanted to lock the door, desperately. But I couldn't risk being thrown out.

I considered trying to find Amleset in the hotel, but that would mean walking through the bar, which was completely unsafe. My only option was to stay awake and fight. Rahel could force me to leave the door open, but she couldn't force me to have sex with strange men.

That night a total of five men wobbled and hobbled their way to my room.

Thankfully each of them was so drunk they could barely stand, making it easy for me to keep them out or fight them off.

By 4:00 a.m., the noise from the bar subsided.

A pulsing fury thumped in my head.

I would wait for it to subside before confronting Rahel.

It took hours, but eventually I calmed down and walked into the main area of the house.

Rahel was sitting, looking over some papers again.

'Good morning, Fiori!' she chimed. 'How did you sleep?'

I shook my head in disbelief. She was acting like absolutely nothing had happened!

'You *know* how I slept,' I said. 'I appreciate your help, but I don't appreciate you trying to sell my body to strangers. If that's how you treat a daughter, I'd hate to see how you treat an enemy.'

Her gasp was a little too loud and lavish. 'Again with the accusations, Fiori? How dare you say such things!'

'I'm accusing you because the men asked for a virgin. They also made reference to a nuns' camp. How would they know this, unless you told them?'

Rahel shrugged her shoulders. 'I don't have time for this, Fiori. I have been nothing but kind to you. I helped secure your release from prison. I've found you a guide. I've given you food, water, and a roof over your head. If you're not happy, you can leave. And remember, this *is* a bar, Fiori. Men will wander around when they're drunk. If you're not comfortable with that, just go.'

That was the problem.

I had nowhere *to* go.

I'd given Rahel nearly all my money. I didn't have access to a phone. I was literally at her mercy.

Without saying another word, I walked back to my room.

I decided to stay away from Rahel as much as possible.

I kept my head low.

I stayed alert.

And I hoped like crazy the guide would come to get me soon.

For the next two days I mainly stayed cooped up in Rahel's bedroom. I tried to nap during the day because I needed my alertness at night. Amazingly, Rahel *still* sent staggering, disorien-

tated men to my room, but thankfully I was able to keep fighting
them off. I don't know how she scammed these men without
retribution from them. They paid their money yet got nothing in
return.

Sometimes I accidentally crossed paths with Rahel during the
day, but I remained businesslike at all times.

I simply waited patiently for news of the guide.

And finally, it came.

'Be ready,' Rahel told me one morning. 'The guide will come
tonight. Meet him in the kitchen at 9:00 p.m.'

The news sent my head into a giddying spin.

I was excited at the possibility of finally crossing the border.

I packed and re-packed.

I paced and re-paced.

It seemed like night time would never come.

And yet when it did, my stomach was in knots.

Who was the guide?

Where was he from?

What future awaited me?

When the guide walked into the kitchen, some of my questions
were answered.

He was a tall, big man with a broad nose, velvety dark skin,
and a mop of matted, hazelnut-coloured hair.

I immediately recognised him as a Kunama man.

The Kunama are one of the indigenous peoples of Eritrea, working predominantly as farmers. They have different features to other Eritreans, particularly their very dark skin.

'I'm Quala,' he said.

Quala spoke to me in basic Tirygani, which was my Eritrean mother tongue, but not his. He spoke a different Eritrean language that I didn't know. As he walked closer, I noticed his eyes were bloodshot.

The redness rattled me.

They made him look aggressive or unstable.

'Hello,' I squeaked.

His eyes flicked this way and that, and he constantly looked over his shoulder.

'Don't ask many questions,' he said. 'Trust me. Follow me. If you trust, if you follow, you will stay alive.'

Don't ask questions?

Follow him?

Trust him?

I had to make a decision about whether it was actually safe to leave with Quala.

Did I think he was a friendly person?

No.

Did I think he had dark intentions?

Honestly, I wasn't sure.

But, did I have any safer options?

Unfortunately not.

With that depressing thought, I ventured with him into the murky night.

He said nothing as we walked, and I wasn't sure whether his silence was a good or bad sign.

After around ninety quiet minutes, we arrived at Quala's home.

It was a small straw hut grouped together with other huts.

Although it was late, Quala's wife was awake. He introduced me to her, as well as his immediate neighbours.

I smiled politely, and they smiled back. They tried to say a few things to me, but couldn't speak Tirygani, so we just had an awkward but friendly exchange.

It was an odd experience, being unable to communicate with fellow Eritreans while in Eritrea. It was like being in a different country altogether.

I remembered from school that the Kunama people are one of nine ethnicities within Eritrea. They have their own language, culture, and traditions. They dance differently, worship differently, dress differently, and even eat different types of food.

I found out quickly about the food.

Quala's wife placed a bowl of soup in front of me.

It looked like a green broth with chunks of meat in it.

The soup was bitter in flavour, and if not for my ravenous hunger, I would have found it difficult to swallow.

I appreciated his wife's hospitality though. Her big, gold nose ring seemed to dance every time she smiled, which was often.

She happily showed me the spot on the floor where I'd sleep. Given the hut was comprised of just one small area, it was kind of her to offer such a generous patch.

I eventually fell asleep and woke up the next morning feeling groggy, but well.

As I stretched my back, Quala said, 'Investigating safety of roads today. See if soldiers at border or not. Stay inside. We could leave in one hour or one month. I will speak to people who have crossed border. Find out more.'

I nodded.

I spent most of my time inside, as requested.

Sometimes I tried communicating with Quala's wife through basic words or sign language, but it was difficult.

I missed communicating, especially with the ones I loved.

I thought of Mum, Dad, and Amanuel, and pangs of sadness squeezed at my chest.

I pushed the thoughts out of my head.

I couldn't afford to lose focus.

And yet, I was losing focus often, mainly because I had no idea when we were leaving.

My one day spent at Quala's home turned into two days, then two days into three.

Quala would come and go as he pleased, doing whatever he did when he left the house.

I found myself pacing like a caged lioness.

Minutes oozed slug-like into the next.

Hours crawled into each other.

Thankfully, early on the fourth morning, Quala said, 'Fiori, we leave right now.'

I wanted to chant to the heavens as though a baby was born. I packed my small bag and stood there, waiting, fidgeting.

'What's wrong?' he asked.

'Nothing,' I reassured. 'I'm just glad we're finally leaving.'

He tilted his head. 'We waited. *Had* to wait. Now is safest time to leave. You have problem with that?'

'No, not at all. I'm just excited.'

He then asked the strangest question. 'You think you better than me, because skin is lighter? You lighter, me darker?'

'No! Of course not.'

'You trust me?' he snapped.

I replied with, 'Yes, of course,' even though I *wanted* to answer with, 'Hell no, not when you blurt out stuff like that!'

He seemed to relax a bit.

'Good. We go,' he said. 'You choose between wheels or hump.'

Hump? Like a piggy back? NOT the journey I signed up for.

He saw my confusion and tried to explain. 'Wheels ... eh ... bike, or you ride on camel. Shared bike takes one day, we pedal. Camel, five days, no pedalling.'

So it was a choice between an animal doing the work, but sitting on that animal for longer—or us doing the work on a bike, but for less time.

The idea of being on a camel as it lurched upward from its sitting position terrified me. Also, the thought of being in Sudan in one day, rather than five, was appealing.

'The bike please,' I said as politely as possible.

'Wear this,' he ordered, throwing me a long white Arab man's dress. 'Abaya. This called abaya. Must look like man. Man and woman cannot cycle in Sudan, only man and man. Wear abaya, look like man.'

He also gave me a scarf. It was the kind of men's scarf that wraps around your head, only revealing your eyes. Both the abaya and scarf were dirty, and I assumed belonged to him.

He then pulled out a woman's abaya.

'Bought this for you,' he said. 'You must wear in Sudan. You must pay for it.'

More payment?

'But I've given most of my money to Rahel for this trip,' I said. 'Can't Rahel pay you? I have very little money left.'

'Rahel no pay for abaya. You pay for abaya, or can't go.'

I sighed.

No payment, no trip to Sudan.

With a heavy heart, I gave him the very last of my money.

He passed me the women's abaya, which I shoved annoyingly into my bag.

At least we were finally ready to go.

Quala pulled the bike out. It was a rickety two-person contraption that looked more like a mode of torture than transport. Quala sat on the front seat and I sat behind him on the second seat.

'Take turns,' he said. 'You pedal thirty minutes. I pedal thirty minutes.'

I agreed, but within seconds of being on the hard seat, I wondered how I would manage for thirty minutes, let alone the full journey of twenty-four hours!

While the pedalling was uncomfortable, it was *nothing* compared to the mental pain Quala was about to put me through.

Away from his home, he felt free to air his real voice.

He started telling me stories ranging from humour to horror.

He made jokes that weren't funny: 'I going to rape you. You be more comfortable on bike after that!'

Laugh. Laugh.

He asked questions to shock and scare: 'You been stabbed? I have knife. Maybe show you what it feels like later?'

Laugh. Laugh.

He told stories that were smothered in thick, dark threats: 'That cemetery there, filled with Eritreans who died making same journey. You probably die too. If not, I bury you alive.'

Laugh. Laugh.

Each time, his laughter became more sinister and cutting.

For some sick reason, Quala wanted to fill me with fear.

It was working!

I honestly thought it was only a matter of time before he'd rape and kill me. I was so convinced I'd die that I even told God I'd be visiting soon.

But then, a thought popped into my head, giving me a glimmer of hope.

Quala could only extort money from my family and me if I was alive, not dead.

Feeling reassured that I probably wouldn't die, I realised the sooner I parted ways with him, the better. So I pedalled hard. I pedalled with fury and fire.

My enthusiastic pedalling and our lack of lengthy breaks paid off.

After twenty-four, back-breaking, thigh-burning, mind-taunting hours, we eventually arrived in the Sudanese town of Kassala.

When I got off the bike, my legs nearly dripped from my hips.

I ached and throbbed from head to toe.

My hands tingled and prickled.

My shoulders hunched and hurt.

But sadly there was zero time to recover. The clock was ticking.

I ducked behind a tree and changed into the female abaya that Quala had sold me.

Meanwhile, he hid the bike in some bushes.

As soon as I changed into the abaya, I caught up to Quala who had started walking.

I walked behind him though, because, as per Sharia law—the Islamic law passed down from the Koran—I couldn't walk beside him in Sudan.

That was fine with me. Keeping my distance from Quala was not a bad thing!

He made his way to a street phone to call my mum for my relatives' address.

He tried to dial the number, but the call wouldn't go through.

Instead of trying again, Quala broke out into a violent sweat.

He looked around, this way and that.

He shuffled and he squirmed.

Then he did something truly unbelievable.

Worried that the Sudanese police would arrest him for being a people smuggler, he ran into the bushes, whispering, 'Don't follow me, I am gone.'

'Quala!' I whisper-shouted back.

But he had melted into the shadows with no concern for my safety or welfare.

To him, the job was done.

But his job *wasn't* done. He hadn't contacted my mum, and I had no idea how to make that call on my own, with the different kind of numbers, not to mention that I had run out of money. He also had not taken me to my Sudanese relatives.

I looked around, feeling completely exposed.

I sat down, shaky.

I wrapped my arms around my hunched body.

It was morning, but still dark.
I felt painfully alone and afraid in this strange, new place.
To survive, I'd need a miracle.
Just as well I looked up to the sky, because there it was.

CHAPTER FOUR

SENSE OF FREEDOM.
SENSE OF LOSS.

The destination may be miles in the distance,

but the next step is always just one foot away.

My miracle was simple, yet profound.

It was a sunrise.

How could a sunrise be a miracle?

Because to me, it was a sign from God.

A glowing sign that I interpreted as, 'You are not alone.'

And what a sign—*what* a sunrise.

It unfurled into the sky like a copper-mottled blossom.

It beamed rays toward me like radiant, outstretched arms.

It laced the clouds with silver linings.

It draped my shoulders with a warm blanket of faith.

It held me close in a reassuring hug. I happily sat in its soft, protective embrace.

Quala may have left me, but God was by my side.

He recharged me. Gave me fuel.

And that fuel powered me to take action.

A simple action.

I stood up.

I put one foot in front of the other.

And I walked.

Slowly at first, tentatively, and then with more confidence.

I had no idea where I was walking to; I just knew I had to move.

I eventually came to a dirt road and a marketplace.

There were dusty buildings and vendor booths surrounded by chattering men setting up for a day of trading.

There was life.

Action.

People.

I was relieved, and yet, I had to be cautious.

To avoid looking out of place, I straightened my shoulders, smiled, and began walking with purpose toward nowhere at all.

My change of posture had a subtle effect on my mood and outlook.

Rather than wrestling with fearful thoughts, I turned my attention outward.

It took a little while, but I eventually stopped drowning in my whirlpool of worries.

I watched and listened.

I delighted in the language. The Sudanese-Arabic words flitted and flew through the air like brightly-coloured kites.

I enjoyed the rhythm of the speech, the way the letter *h* burst and blossomed within every sentence.

Over the next few hours, I walked into mazes of streets, labyrinths of lanes, and vein-like paths that pulsed deep into the heart of Kassala city.

I walked and walked, until eventually, I ran out of energy.

My purposeful steps limped into a stroll.

My gaze became blank.

My posture screamed, 'I'm alone! I'm lost! I'm vulnerable!'

My thoughts collapsed inward again, and imploded.

Sensing my depleted energy, men started smiling, saying, '*Aww ya jemila, ya hilwa, ya Jedid.*'

The words leapt friskily from their lips.

I figured they were being flirtatious, and I was right. (Later I'd find out they were saying, 'Oh how lovely you are; how beautiful you are.')

It struck me as odd that men were so flirtatious despite the strictness of Sharia law, which included restrictions regarding public affection and rigid rules pertaining to women's clothing.

Something else struck me. A fearful thought that pierced through my mind like a lightning spear.

Sex slaves.

I remembered stories I'd heard back home about Sudanese men capturing Eritrean girls and keeping them as sex slaves. These girls would be held captive and repeatedly raped, either by one owner, or by groups of different men.

Fear instantly snatched the breath from my body.

I could barely inhale. Scarcely think. Hardly move.

And yet, I had to.

I couldn't stop.

I kept limping forward on shaky legs.

If I collapsed, I would be defenceless.

Later on it would be dark. The stunning sunrise that gave me so much hope would eventually sprawl tiredly into the night.

I somehow kept hobbling for one more hour, putting one unsteady foot in front of the other.

Moving was good, but where was I moving *to*?

At some point, I would *have* to stop.

Then what?

I couldn't think of the outcome.

I had to be strong.

I had to survive. Not just for me, but for Amanuel too.

Keep going! Keep going!

It was just at that determined moment that something caught my eye.

Or should I say, some*one*.

There was a man in a front yard, sawing a piece of wood.

This man looked Eritrean to me. He had a straight, brown nose, and smooth, chiselled cheeks.

I crossed the road, slowly, tentatively.

I inched my way over.

He looked up.

I forced myself to speak, though my voice was just a murmur. 'Excuse me. Are you Eritrean?'

He stopped, put his saw down, and looked at me kindly.

'Did you just arrive?' he asked, his voice concerned and tender.

I collapsed. A sob that had been bubbling deep within my stomach erupted and tumbled from my throat. A dam burst in my heart. I couldn't believe that I had found a person who spoke my language, who was from my country.

Relief flooded over me faster than my tears could keep up.

The carpenter knelt down alongside me and put his hand gently around my shoulder. 'I'm glad you are safe now, my daughter.'

Eventually my shoulders stopped rattling from the sobs.

Actually, as I adjusted to the fact that I was no longer in danger, my sobs turned into smiles, and those smiles turned into an embarrassed giggle.

The carpenter laughed too. 'Let's get up.'

Amidst my river of tears, I felt reborn.

In my darkest hour, I found someone to help me.

For the first time ever, I felt free.

Free of war and violence and atrocities. Free of expectations and one-way roads.

I felt as though now, I could truly defy my destiny.

I could finally see the world around me.

Everything looked and smelled like freedom.

An ambitious force welled and whirled within me, making me want to scream with joy.

I restrained myself; after all, I'd been gifted a saviour in the form of a lovely Eritrean man. I certainly didn't want to scare him off with hysterics.

The carpenter took me into his home and gave me some water. He said, 'Before it's dark, I will take you to an Eritrean family who welcomes new arrivals. You can stay with them until you are ready. But first, have you called your parents?'

'Unfortunately, no. I ran out of money.'

He picked up a small pouch filled with coins. 'We will call them at the street phone on the way. Your parents will be worried sick.'

He was right, of course.

'Are you okay?!' Mum blurted out as soon as she picked up the phone. 'Fiori, where are you? What happened? I was expecting a call sooner. Amleset told me you were imprisoned and then released into a good woman's care? Are you okay? Did you find a guide? Are you in Sudan?'

'Yes, I'm in Sudan,' I reassured, unable to answer all her questions.

Mum chanted to the heavens, singing praises of gratitude to God. She was practically frantic with delight. 'I can't believe it. You are safe! My daughter is safe!'

'I'm safe, Mum. I'm sorry—the guide tried to phone you when we got to Kassala a few hours ago, but the call didn't go through. He panicked and abandoned me.'

'He *abandoned* you? Who is this man?!'

'It doesn't matter, Mum. He's gone now. I wandered the streets, and I found a nice person. He's going to take me to an Eritrean family.'

Mum calmed down. 'Okay. That's good. That's very good. So you don't need the details of our relatives in Sudan? I'm glad, because I've been asking around but cannot locate them. I was going to suggest you staying at a hotel, and I'd send money, but staying with a family is much better. Can I speak to the man you're with?'

'Of course.'

I passed the phone to the carpenter; he smiled and took it.

My mum was so loud and happy that I could actually hear what she was saying through the mouthpiece. She was asking who he was, and could he please look after me like I was his own daughter. She told him she'd send money as soon as possible.

'You daughter is very safe,' he reassured. 'She will continue to be in safe hands with the family nearby. I will keep checking on her as well. You have nothing to worry about.'

Mum kept talking excitedly, her voice like a hula hoop twirling around him. No doubt she could have spoken for hours, but she knew we were running out of coins. Toward the end of her conversation she said, 'I know this call must be costing a lot, but may I please talk to Fiori again briefly?'

'Yes, here she is,' he replied.

The carpenter passed the phone back. Mum's voice was still fluttery, but definitely more settled.

'The worst is behind you, Fiori,' she said. 'You are a thoughtful girl. Now, more than ever, you need to continue being a thoughtful and kind person. When you move in with the family, be sure to help with the house chores and do your share in every way possible. You are a lucky girl, Fiori. You are the daughter of many great generations of women—grandmothers and great-grandmothers who were honest, Godly women. It was their collective prayers that kept you safe, and will continue to keep you safe. Do you understand?'

Mum's words poured into my soul like a rich soup of warm hugs. They filtered through my body, nourishing every cell. 'Yes Mum, I understand.'

'I know you'll want to work soon,' Mum continued. 'Be smart about money. Make it honourably, keep it safely, and spend it wisely. It is a necessary part of your life. It can open doors, but it should never be your *reason* for living.'

I was nodding, grateful for the priceless advice, but conscious of the diminishing coins. 'Mum, I agree with everything you're saying, and I'm sorry to rush, but I have to go now. This phone line is going to cut off at any moment.'

Mum spoke fast. 'Fiori, when you're settled, contact me with the address. I'll send some money to help you get on your feet, and for the carpenter too. I love you, Fiori. Goodbye!'

'Thank you Mum, I love you too.'

As I bid Mum farewell, I felt as though I'd touched the wings of an angel.

I savoured the divine feeling.

I felt the sun rise in my soul.

I felt its light shine within me like rays of hope.

I stood taller and prouder.

The strength of my mother and grandmothers, of all women, radiated within me.

It was a new day.

A new life.

A new chance at freedom.

An eagle stirred within.

The Eritrean family I lived with was warm and friendly, as most Eritrean families are.

With Mum's words echoing in my ears, I happily did my fair share of chores in return for their hospitality.

I stayed with them for a couple of weeks before travelling to Port Sudan, a city located approximately seven hours from Kassala, where I stayed with relatives.

I also enrolled in high school, supporting myself by working as a cleaner.

Being back in school was an uplifting and exciting experience, but there were many tasks to do in order to settle in. One of them was organising a photograph for my student identification.

Easy enough.

I went to a local photo shop and had my photograph taken, and was told to return in three days to pick up my four photos.

As instructed, I returned in a few days, paid my money, collected my packet of photographs, and left the store.

The package felt a bit bulky though, so I sat down at a nearby bench to check the envelope.

Huh?!

There were loads of photos of me inside, all the same photo, but different sizes.

I decided to count them.

Seven hundred!

Seven hundred photos!

I walked straight back into the store.

The assistant at the counter smirked. 'I was expecting you back. The extra photos are complimentary from the guy who works here as our photo developer.'

I felt a smile roll across my face like a long, welcoming carpet. 'I see. Well that's nice of him. Where is he? Can I talk to him?'

'Sorry, no,' he said, laughing. 'I've told you as much as I can. I don't think he'd want me to say any more than I already have!'

'If that's the case, please pass on my thanks.' I then walked out with a spring in my step, delighted by the gesture.

The thought stayed with me all day, but eventually got buried under schoolwork and my endless to-do list.

A few days later, though, I got a call.

'Hi, this is Yonas. I'm the guy from the photo shop.'

'Oh,' I said, my heart deciding to become that of a racehorse.

'I can't talk for long, but I was wondering if you'd be interested in catching up for a coffee?'

'Yes, that sounds great,' I answered immediately. I could tell just from his voice that he was young like me, and, I was flattered by his romantic and creative photo gesture. I wanted to meet the person behind the plan.

We arranged a date, time, and place to meet, and the call ended.

As soon as I saw Yonas the next day, my heart raced even faster. His hair was a field of chestnut spirals, his eyes were deep and thoughtful, his eyebrows were lush, and his mile-wide smile was warm and welcoming.

I didn't waste any time on pleasantries. I giggled and said, 'Why on earth did you print seven hundred photos of me?'

'You are so beautiful!' he replied. 'Four photos wasn't enough. Even seven hundred wasn't enough, but it's all I could afford. I thought it would make my point though.'

Point definitely taken! His confidence was mesmerising.

We talked about the photos for a bit longer before delving into where we were born, what our life stories were, and what our hopes and dreams were.

Our conversation flowed like a perfect stream, fresh and invigorating.

It continued to flow for hours.

After that initial meeting, we met again the following Friday, and the Friday after that.

Even though we could only catch up one afternoon per week due to our busy schedules, it was always a relaxed, wonderful afternoon.

Before long, we grew closer, and eventually became boyfriend and girlfriend.

We continued seeing each other on Fridays, which was definitely the highlight of my hectic weeks. Yonas had a poetic way with words, and I loved his caring, attentive nature.

I loved being his girlfriend.

But as wonderful as our relationship was, I decided I wanted to move almost 700 kilometres (over 400 miles) away, to Khartoum, the capital of Sudan. Khartoum had more jobs and opportunities, especially with international companies.

I knew I would miss Yonas, but my original plan was always to seek out the most fulfilling jobs.

When I broke the news to Yonas, his response was expected and understandable.

'Why would you want to leave? We've only just started our relationship. We're so happy.'

I wasn't sure how to reply. I mean, it *was* special. It just wasn't enough on its own. I needed more. That's why I'd refused to be a child bride. That's why I'd defied my destiny. I needed more knowledge, more education, more experiences, more opportunities.

'We *are* happy,' I reassured him. 'But there are not enough good jobs for me here in Port Sudan. We can still be girlfriend and boyfriend; we just won't see each other every Friday. We can talk on the phone though.'

'It's not the same thing!'

We went around in circles for a while. First Yonas wanted to break up, then he didn't, then he did.

It was a confusing time. I don't blame Yonas, because I was confused about our relationship too.

I was crystal clear about my decision to move though. From my first scary day in Sudan when I felt reborn, I had had a powerful drive within me. It was like an eagle was in my soul. I literally travelled with my feet above the ground.

I no longer had limits.

I no longer walked a worn path.

I could make my *own* roads.

And those roads, for now, led to Khartoum.

Khartoum was a big, busy city with wide roads, a swarm of cars, and hives of dusty, brown buildings.

I saw people walking with purpose. I too wanted to walk like them, to places of relevance and importance.

I saw stairs leading to buildings. I too wanted to climb them, to positions of challenge and enjoyment.

As for opportunities, they seemed to be everywhere.

I could almost *feel* them in my bones.

I wanted to find them, grab them, conquer them.

All I had to do was get started.

So that's what I did. I got started.

I found a small room to rent. And when I say 'small,' I mean *small*—smaller than the size of a car, with only a single bed mattress on the floor.

I found a job as a maid.

I located a place to learn Arabic.

Quickly, I fell into a productive routine where I'd work hard during the day, and work equally hard during Arabic lessons at night. Rather than being two separate entities, the activities meshed together perfectly. I'd learn Arabic in the evening and practice it during the day with the locals.

Learning the language was difficult.

The easy and more relaxing option was to just speak Tirygani to other Eritreans in Khartoum. It was safe. It was comfortable. But it would also have kept me trapped and tethered.

Arabic was the tool that would help me fly. Help me assimilate and grow.

Sometimes, when I tried to say a sentence in Arabic, it was like running across a road covered in banana peels. And yet, while slipping and sliding, stumbling and fumbling, people often smiled and helped me get to the other side. We made the journey together, because I was willing to take the first step.

My long-distance relationship with Yonas was all about steps too.

One step forward, two steps back. Maybe not for him, but definitely for me. At first I loved speaking with him once a week, but after several weeks, I felt drained. Yonas had no intention of coming to Khartoum, and I had no intention of returning to Port

Sudan. So a little voice in my head kept saying, 'Where is this relationship going?'

I was too exhausted to answer the question, but my actions did the talking.

More and more I kept the conversations short.

More and more I'd tell Yonas I was busy, that I couldn't talk.

More and more, I focused solely on life in Khartoum.

There was a disconnect. He could sense it. I could sense it. But we travelled along, not discussing the elephant in the room.

It didn't help that we were so caught up with our respective lives.

For me, life was a whirlwind of language studies and work.

In fact, after intense evening classes and practising the language daily, my Arabic skills improved to the point where I could start applying for more challenging work.

I started asking people if they knew of other jobs, and soon, opportunities came my way.

Within a short space of time, I resigned from being a maid and started working as a receptionist and all-rounder in two separate businesses, as well as taking on computer studies.

If I thought my life was busy before, I was in for a surprise!

I worked from 7:00 a.m. to 3:00 p.m. in an internet café. I'd then dart over to an education block to study basic computer skills from 3:30 p.m. to 4:00 p.m. Then I'd walk next door to a Sudanese restaurant to work from 4:00 p.m. to midnight.

It was a long, exhausting day, but to a certain extent, I was used to it. I had been working long hours since I was a child. I'd helped manage my parents' grocery store at such a young age. Once I started school, I attended classes during the day and headed straight to one of my parents' businesses in the afternoon, working several hours before returning home to eat and study.

Working in these new Khartoum positions kept me buzzing along. I had an excited energy that powered me forward every moment of every day.

In the midst of this crazy schedule, I spoke to Yonas even less.

Now, he was genuinely concerned.

He felt me drifting further away.

He was worried, and decided to do something about it. Despite being uninterested in moving to Khartoum originally, he decided it was the only way to make our relationship work.

I was excited about his decision, because the long-distance relationship had depleted me. And I knew that being together would be just like old times.

And it was.

As soon as he got off the bus, we hugged and laughed and talked.

We were together again, and it felt right.

But we still took our relationship slowly. Rather than move in with me, Yonas lived with a few of his friends who went to the university in Khartoum.

We managed to spend time with each other amidst my busy schedule, but little did we know, things were about to get even busier!

Thanks to my parents and their businesses, I developed a keen entrepreneurial streak. This streak came in handy because after three months at the Sudanese restaurant, my boss got a working visa for the United Kingdom.

This got me thinking.

What if *I* took over the restaurant?

Crazy?

Maybe.

But in a quiet moment, I sat down with my boss and said, 'I'd like to take over the restaurant in your absence. I'll pay all the expenses, and we can split the profits straight down the middle.'

My boss nodded and didn't register one shred of shock. Most people would have immediately scoffed at such an offer from a sixteen-year-old girl.

'You've proved your worth and loyalty from your very first day,' he said. 'I'll think about it.'

Yes! He was going to consider it!

To me, the business proposal was a win-win for both of us. He would enjoy a stream of income while not having to physically be there (back then I didn't know it was called 'passive income'), while I would enjoy the challenge of running the restaurant.

And what a challenge I envisioned it would be.

I didn't want to just answer phones, I wanted to answer to myself.

I didn't want to just steer the ship, I wanted to plot its course.

Failure or success, I wanted it to be on me.

No excuses. No regrets. One hundred percent responsibility.

I hoped and prayed he would agree.

Much to my relief, after a week of thinking about, it he *did* agree. He also gave me more details. He told me I'd have a contact in Sudan—Jamal—who would collect the earnings, look over the books, and help me if needed. But he insisted that I was the manager, and that I would be responsible for everything.

Within a fortnight the owner left, and I officially became the manager!

Every cell in my body seemed to fizz with excitement.

I managed five full-time employees as well as a handful of casual staff.

The team became like my family. I respected that they were older and wiser, and they respected that I poured all my time and energy into making the restaurant better each day. It was a nurturing, appreciative environment.

There was one issue—I wanted to keep my job at the internet café because it gave me excellent experience, while also paying well.

But this meant I'd need to find someone to manage the restaurant in the mornings.

It seemed my first challenge as manager would be recruiting a new staff member, and not just any staff member either. The person would need to be responsible, honest, and hardworking because I was trusting them with a restaurant that had been trusted to *me*.

That's when I thought of Yonas.

He was definitely honest and responsible, and as for hardworking, his work ethic was identical to mine.

It was a choice that seemed too good to be true. But, I wasn't sure if he'd be keen to work in a restaurant, or more importantly, whether he'd be comfortable having me as his boss.

When I proposed the idea, though, he was delighted: 'Of course I'm interested, Fiori. As an added bonus I will see you throughout the day. It's perfect.'

It *was* perfect. Yonas started the next day, and not surprisingly, he immediately became a wonderful addition to the team. The staff loved him because he had a masterful way of learning from them while simultaneously boosting their confidence. The customers loved him because he was endlessly joyful and accommodating.

Yonas successfully ran the restaurant in the mornings, and as soon as my internet café shift ended at 3:00 p.m., I headed straight to the restaurant. Unfortunately I had to drop my daily computer course, but it was a small price to pay in order to work in such a friendly and invigorating environment.

It was also a fun environment! My Arabic was only semi-fluent, so the restaurant staff would sometimes laugh uncontrollably at my incorrect words and sentences.

Those fun times certainly helped break up the long, busy days. Our kitchen was particularly hectic at night because Sudanese customers ordered a *lot* of food. It wasn't uncommon for two people to order up to six dishes. It seems excessive, but either they'd enjoy the dishes themselves, or, happily invite passing strangers to eat with them purely out of a sense of joy and generosity.

I saw this giving spirit everywhere in Sudan, not just in our restaurant. I saw it on the streets, in shops, and on public transport.

In fact, here's a scenario I personally witnessed a few times.

During each bus ride, a conductor would walk down the aisle to collect money from passengers. If a passenger on the bus was struggling financially, the passenger would say, '*Maondi*,' which is, 'I don't have the money.'

In most other countries you'd be thrown off the bus or get a fine. Not in Sudan. Most of the time, the collector would allow the person to ride for free. If he didn't, all hell would break loose. Other passengers would stand up and shame the conductor, saying, 'This person has no money, have some mercy!' Or, 'What sort of a man makes a poor person walk?!'

The conductor would almost always back down and let the passenger ride for free.

This generosity of spirit was everywhere, and I loved the way the essence of goodness flowed through our restaurant in particular, like the fragrant steam from frying spices. It really did make the long shifts much shorter, and the hard work much easier.

For Yonas and I, the hard work didn't drive us apart; it brought us closer together.

We spent hours together at the restaurant, and during rare free time, we'd hang out with each other, or his friends. Though very quickly, his friends became my friends too. We were a close-knit group.

Many areas of my life were blissful.

But sadly, not all.

There were a few areas of huge concern.

For example, I often ended up in jail!

Yes ... jail ... the one place I did *not* want to visit again.

The reason for my regular incarcerations was because every time I saw Eritrean people on the street, regardless of gender, I'd kiss them three times on the cheeks as per our cultural greeting. But because of Sudan's Sharia Law, I wasn't even allowed to stand with a man for long, let alone kiss him on the cheek in public! But all my life I'd kissed people on the cheek, so it was a tough habit to break, especially when I'd get so excited seeing someone from Eritrea. I was also put in jail a few times because my head scarf kept slipping off.

Thankfully, I was often released with a warning, or, I'd have to bribe my way out.

While those incarcerations were a source of frustration and disappointment, there were other bigger concerns.

Years earlier, Eritrea had been at war with Sudan, and during that time the Sudanese government deported all Eritreans.

The fact that such a situation could occur again was terrifying to me. I could be jailed if I was returned.

As I thought more and more about the possibility of such a deportation, I grew uneasy and restless.

Additionally, although the majority of Sudanese people were generous, welcoming, polite, and hospitable, I would periodically hear of an Eritrean female going missing, never to be seen or heard of again.

Although I didn't live in great fear, I experienced an *undercurrent* of fear.

It was a fear that made me look over my shoulder, swipe at shadows, and sometimes restrict my movements.

In war-torn Eritrea, death was all around.

It was in the corpses that baked in the sun.

It was in the blood that streaked the streets.

It whispered in the wind and shouted from the mountains.

It was literally everywhere.

I didn't want it to be in Khartoum too.

When I tried to imagine my future in Sudan, it was always shrouded in uncertainty.

Over time, the joy I felt at being in Sudan retreated into nervousness and doubt.

Eventually, sadly, I came to the realisation that I couldn't build a safe life in Sudan.

I spoke to Yonas about my concerns one day, explaining to him that it was probably safest if I left.

His response was fast: 'Then I am leaving with you.'

There was no two ways about it.

He was coming.

I hugged him. For the first time since leaving Eritrea, this was a journey I'd be taking with someone else, which brought me comfort.

During quiet moments, I started looking for ways to depart that didn't require legal papers, huge amounts of money, or enormous wait times. If there was a proper channel, I would have taken it, but logistically I didn't have the papers, nor copious amounts of money.

Eventually, one of the ways I discovered we could escape to Libya was through the Libyan Desert.

Once there, we could either stay in Libya, if it was safe, or cross the Mediterranean Sea into Italy if it wasn't.

Emotionally and physically, the journey to Libya would be hard.

People had died on the hot, harsh trip.

We could die too.

It was a big risk.

For me, though, taking risks seemed to be the thread that sewed together significant pieces of my life. Each section of time was a new patch of cloth; and each colourful, jagged thread was the risk that connected it to the rest of the quilt.

It was time to lengthen my quilt.

It was time to take another risk.

Although it was the right decision, I was dreading talking to Jamal about leaving the restaurant, but knew I had to bite the bullet.

I organised a meeting with him, and said, 'Jamal, I'm sorry. I've made the decision to resign; I need to stop managing the restaurant.'

Jamal raised a brow. 'Why? I thought you enjoyed the role. And you've done such an excellent job, especially for someone so young.'

'Thank you so much, I've loved every moment,' I said, 'but actually, *because* I'm so young, I just want to take some time out to enjoy life.'

I couldn't tell him the real reason, because escaping into Libya was illegal. Only Yonas and I could know.

Jamal laughed. 'Bullshit!'

'What? Why do you say that?'

'Fiori, you're a workaholic! You'd go crazy not working. What's the real reason?'

'I told you. I just want to enjoy life.'

Jamal wasn't stupid. He knew that many people used Sudan as a transit city before launching to other places, often illegally. Although it wasn't originally my intention to use Sudan as a transit city, I was definitely using it as one now, but I couldn't tell Jamal that.

He nodded sceptically but thankfully stopped his line of questioning. 'If you want to enjoy life, Fiori, I can only wish you the best.'

I finally unclenched my wringing hands.

Our meeting wasn't over though. We had a lot of business-related matters to discuss.

Having occasional, one-on-one meetings with Jamal invigorated me. Nutting out issues and brainstorming ideas was both exciting and rewarding. I wished I could do more of it. (Without realising it, a tiny germ of a seed was planted—one I would carefully tend and watch flourish years down the road.)

Once the official business was taken care of, I kept working at the restaurant to serve out my notice.

On my last day, I said my final farewells to the staff. They remained confused about why I was leaving, and were sad to see me go.

I was sad too, incredibly sad.

A few days later, perhaps knowing the risks that lay ahead, Yonas and I went to a studio to have professional photographs taken to commemorate our time in Sudan. No matter what happened in life, we'd always be together in the photos.

And life, not surprisingly, was moving at a fast pace. Once we decided to leave, we arranged the journey quickly.

Before long, the afternoon of departure arrived.

We met secretly at a house, carrying a small bag filled with dried food and bottles of water.

The house was crammed with people, and we ended up living with these same people for a few days, until it was safe to travel.

It turns out, being tightly packed was good preparation for the actual journey, because we all had to fit into three open-backed four-wheel-drive vehicles.

On the day of travelling, everyone smiled politely at first, but the smiles soon disappeared as we filed into the vehicles. Each four-wheel drive had to fit forty-five passengers.

Forty-five.

This meant people had to sit on each other's laps, on each other's legs, on each other's arms, and any other available space!

Some people hung off the edges, and we *all* hung on for dear life.

As our four-wheel drive began to move, its outward groans seemed to match my inward ones. The small amount of food and water we brought was on the vehicle's roof alongside everyone else's, adding to the heavy weight on the suspension.

The heat pulsing off our bodies created a furnace in an already hot, desert environment.

Sweat trickled down my back and created a snakes-and-ladders game that I was quickly losing.

The lack of personal space sometimes made me gasp for air.

Although it wasn't exceedingly hot, the sun still sizzled and fizzled into the sky each morning, relentlessly sucking moisture from our bodies throughout the day.

Dehydration quickly took hold.

Our heads throbbed. Our bodies slumped.

The conditions didn't just affect us humans; the poorly-serviced vehicles broke down every few hours.

No matter whose car broke down, though, the others had to stop so all three drivers could assist with getting the engine running again. This meant a huge blowout in our supposed five-day timeline.

Five days stretched into ten days. Ten days into twenty.

During yet another breakdown on the *twenty-third* day, I looked over at Yonas, my heart sinking.

As usual, the drivers fiddled with the engine, pressing this, jiggling that. As usual, the engine neighed like a horse, never kicking over into a growl.

I rolled my eyes.

Different day. Same delay.

By this stage, all the food had run out, and water was strictly rationed. We were literally getting only a few sips of water every few hours.

At ration time, we'd line up. People's rage was as red and angry as their rough, dry throats. Some jumped the queue, while others snatched bottles to share with their group. Whenever this happened, arguments exploded into the air like malfunctioning firecrackers. But like all fireworks, they eventually fizzled out. In their wake lay the burnt debris of sadness and desperation.

Thankfully, there were additional food sources in the desert. The drivers sometimes went out to kill and cook their own animal, but they'd only take people with them who could pay extra.

I wasn't surprised the drivers charged people for food, but I *was* surprised they didn't at least give a small amount to those who needed it most. Those needy people lay on the ground, their eyes sunken, their lips swollen, their skin shrivelled. They looked as though they were close to dying, yet got nothing.

I'd seen dying people before, from the time I was a child, right through to the hundreds of bloodied soldiers in the military hospital. But seeing *these* men and women seemed to flip a switch in me, an angry switch that had never been flipped before.

A fury burned deep inside that was hotter than any desert temperature.

It bubbled like a volcano, causing molten sweat to erupt from my pores.

'Why?' I wondered.

Why must we jump through dangerous hoops to enjoy freedom and safety?

Why must atrocities and injustices be normal occurrences in countries such as mine?

Why must power struggles at high levels create hell for all of us below?

Why must I leave the ones I love—my parents and brother—to enjoy basic liberties?

Why?

Why?!

WHY?

Yonas offered support, but I shrugged off his affection.

What was the point of love in a world filled with hate?

I turned all of Yonas's positive attributes into negative ones, because *I* was consumed with negativity.

Yonas asked me what was wrong, but how could I explain something that I didn't understand myself? Something toxic and irrational.

Even when the four-wheel drive was fixed, I wasn't relieved or happy.

I was seething.

Why so many breakdowns?

Why weren't the vehicles serviced more?

Why did we have to sit on top of each other again?

Why did I have to escape?

Why couldn't I just feel safe and settled?

I stewed in my own sweat and rage for the last leg of the journey.

The trip that was meant to take five days ended up taking a torturous twenty-four.

It's little wonder that, tragically, three people died on the final stretch.

Equally terrible, their bodies were flung from the vehicles to reduce weight. Tossed onto the sand like pieces of garbage.

Any of those people could have been me, or Yonas.

Yet, we'd somehow arrived safely in Libya.

We'd *actually* arrived.

Alive.

It was time for the drivers to drop us off. They did this five kilometres from the city, and told us to run.

It's amazing how, despite our food and water deprivation, we instantly moved into gear.

With nerves firing through our bodies, we scattered and spread.

My anger temporarily burnt away as we tried to find energy to dash.

Yonas and I were with a small group of others. We all picked up the pace as we neared the city. We knew we'd have to filter into the streets quickly and quietly; otherwise, we'd be picked up by authorities.

We stepped softly.

We crept secretly.

And when safe to do so, we whisked into shops to exchange money and buy supplies.

In the shops, we saw other Eritrean groups who had travelled with us. They'd kept a low profile too, but had gathered important information from Eritreans in Libya.

Apparently Tripoli, Libya's capital, was the safest place to live and work.

We spoke directly to other Eritreans in Libya, who confirmed this.

Tripoli it was, then.

Being at a border town, guides milled around constantly. They were easy to find, or they found you first.

We found one within minutes.

This particular guide advised us that travelling to Tripoli would involve hiding in a secret compartment at the bottom of his truck, which would be lined with hay.

It didn't sound appealing in the slightest, but we didn't have many transport choices.

Yonas and I discussed the idea with each other, and decided it was probably our best option.

We followed the guide to his location, and got into his truck. The truck had a false bottom, and we each crawled into the secret compartment. It was dark down there, with only slivers of light streaming in through the vents.

As the truck started moving, we were relieved to begin the journey, but due to the cramped conditions, instantly couldn't wait for it to end.

When we neared each checkpoint, the truck slowed down, and we'd hear muffled talking.

Sometimes the checkpoint guard circled the truck, round and round, like a tourniquet.

Our hearts would beat so loudly we thought the collective banging would reveal our location.

We'd stay still.

We'd hold our breath.

We'd perspire.

We'd listen carefully to doors opening.

To voices raising.

The butterflies in our stomachs would try to escape, only settling when the truck rumbled away without incident.

For three days and nights we stayed in that compartment.

When we needed to pee, we'd urinate in bottles.

When the bottles overflowed, the pee would spill down our legs and clothes, onto the truck floor.

The acidic stench from the urine practically peeled the skin from my nostrils.

When we eventually arrived in Tripoli, fresh air never smelt so good.

With sore backs and dead legs from days of crouching, we hobbled out of the truck and stretched our crooked spines. There was little time for yoga though. We had to focus on our next task, which was finding an Eritrean person. As a people, most Eritreans are like a big family, helping each other no matter what the location, providing information, and even offering a place to sleep.

We found an Eritrean man fairly quickly. As expected, he happily offered his home for the night, which we gratefully and enthusiastically accepted.

The next morning—with a good night's sleep under our belt, fresh clothes, and full stomachs—Yonas and I went out to find a cheap place to rent.

Finding a place to live was relatively easy, but finding a place in *society* was much harder. To the Libyans, we were dark-skinned invaders bringing crime to their country and stealing their jobs.

I hated walking down the street. It's as though we were criminals who had just committed heinous crimes.

People gaped. Glared.

They cursed.

Hissed.

Swore.

Grunted.

This prompted us to huddle close together. Heads low.

On buses we'd sit at the back.

One time, something truly awful happened.

A man spat a glob of saliva on my ankle!

I quickly wiped it away with the other foot.

But I couldn't wipe away the shame.

The soul-destroying shame.

The shame of being seen as worthless, as the lowest of the low.

That shame leaves a scar.

A scar that made me feel like, *I was the scar*.

I was a disease. A filthy, disgusting disease.

Over time, my shoulders slumped over my body.

My eyes dropped to the ground.

And there, they stayed.

The persecution was incessant and everywhere. Day in, day out.

The taunts and terror sucked me of confidence, worth, and joy.

Ironically, we'd left Sudan to find safety, only to walk into the razored arms of racism.

While the danger in Sudan was murky and unpredictable, the danger in Libya was clear and continual.

Despite the racism, I was given work at an internet café, which was a relief because we needed the money.

But no one would employ Yonas.

At the same time as I found the job, sadly, I found my anger again.

The venom that others yelled at me was like fuel spitting on glowing embers.

The fire in the pit of my stomach found life again: bigger, brighter, bolder. It incinerated any shred of positivity, which in turn incinerated my love for Yonas.

Yonas remained loving. He continued laughing. He kept hoping. He was being the beautiful, optimistic man I'd initially fallen in love with. He was doing nothing wrong—he was simply being positive.

But to me, at that time, it was infuriating.

I wished he could be angry too.

I wished that he'd allow fury to tangle him, to squeeze all optimism from his heart.

His joy was like a sharp pebble in my shoe. I needed to empty it, and to then continue walking alone.

Although he'd done nothing wrong, I couldn't control the way I was feeling. I realised it was unfair to string Yonas along when I no longer loved him.

He deserved respect.

He deserved the truth.

So, I did something I never thought I'd do. I broke off our relationship. In the process, I broke his heart.

'Fiori,' he said, 'once our circumstances change, so too will your feelings for me.'

He genuinely believed that.

See? Beautiful and optimistic.

But *I* didn't believe it.

What Yonas knew, is that I was in a terrible mental place. A place both black with bleakness and red with rage.

I think for that reason, he agreed to sever our romantic relationship for that moment in time.

Instead, he focused on our current dire situation.

We'd only planned to stay in Libya if it was safe, and because it wasn't, we considered the option of travelling to the nearest country—Italy.

However, this was an expensive journey by boat, at a time when neither of us had much money.

Yet, it was our only option, so we *had* to find money.

Memories of Mum's conversation swirled through my mind. I worked hard and honourably for every cent I made. I saved it carefully and spent it wisely. Yet, here I was, in a position of having to put my hand out.

It's not a position I ever wanted to be in.

I needed American dollars, and because the Eritrean Nafka at that time wasn't worth much when converted, I called overseas

relatives rather than my Eritrean family. Unfortunately, this
wasn't a fruitful exercise. I was totally disheartened by their lack
of interest. None of them could rummage through their memories
to find a shred of empathy. They had all left Eritrea for the same
reasons we had, and they had all endured pain and suffering.

But they were safe now.

They had money.

They had freedom.

That's all that mattered.

I felt demoralised. It made me question people's humanity even
more.

It added fuel to my fire.

I called Mum, as I did regularly, and as expected, she
generously offered to send Eritrean Nafka, which unfortunately
wouldn't help. I told her I loved her, and that I'd find a solution
soon.

But I actually had no idea what to do. We had a desert behind
us, an ocean in front of us, and a sea of angry Libyans around us.

There seemed to be no way of moving forward.

Yonas was in the same position. In fact, at the same time as I
was calling relatives, he was also reaching out to family. He called
two different uncles living in the United States and explained the
situation to them.

Their responses were quite different to my own relatives'. They
didn't want him to be persecuted or in danger. They simply asked
where to send the money.

I was thrilled for Yonas. He'd found his immediate ticket out of Libya, and I knew I'd eventually get out too. After all, I had found a job working at the internet café, and even if it took a couple of years, I knew I'd one day save up the money to escape.

But Yonas had other ideas.

'Fiori,' he said, 'I'd like to pay for your journey.'

I shook my head. 'No. I can't and won't accept that. But thank you.'

Not surprisingly, because Yonas was a calm and logical person, he put aside our relationship to focus purely on the current situation. Even if we weren't bound by romantic love, we were still bound by friendship love.

'There's no way I'm leaving without you, Fiori. If you stay, I stay.'

What?

No!

I didn't want him to stay! I wanted him to get away from these wretched circumstances just as much as I wanted to myself.

'I mean it,' he said. 'I won't leave without you.'

The truth sizzled in his determined gaze.

Eventually—reluctantly, but gratefully—I accepted his generous gift. It was one of the hardest things I've ever done, particularly as we were no longer boyfriend and girlfriend.

We hugged.

Two friends.

Another journey.

'We need to start planning,' Yonas said, wasting no time.

He was right; the journey required a lot of organisation.

Due to the horrific stories we'd heard about guides who scammed people, we decided to travel to Italy without their help. Instead, we quickly had meetings with other Eritreans who wanted to flee. We discussed our options with the group, and we all decided to pool our meagre resources to buy a boat and life jackets. (I use the term 'boat' loosely, it was an open inflatable rubber dinghy with a small motor!)

We then found an Eritrean sailor who would join and guide us, in return for free passage.

We set a date, and when the night of the voyage eventually arrived, we met quietly under the cover of darkness.

We were concerned there'd be difficult times ahead.

We were right to worry.

CHAPTER FIVE

SINK OR SWIM

———◆———

Better to surrender to immediate uneasiness,

than to be prisoner to later resentment.

The night of our escape, I shivered.

From fear, partly.

From the cold, mostly.

The icy wind burrowed into my bones. It whispered in my ears. It told me secrets I chose not to hear.

So I focused on heat.

I visualised sunny days ahead, and a bright future.

As soon as I did this, surprisingly, I felt slightly warmer.

Not hot, just less cold.

So I continued.

I thought less about the current negatives and more about the future positives. I could do this now that I was no longer consumed with anger. I had become so weary of being bitter, and knew that it wasn't serving me; I just needed to let go of it. And particularly in contrast to my current awful situation with the local people and lack of support from relatives, Yonas was a shining example that the world certainly wasn't all bad.

These positive thoughts poured warm ladles of optimism into my body.

As I looked up, the sky twinkled with possibilities and sparkled with hope. At a certain angle, some of the stars winked at me, like loving grandmothers and great-grandmothers might do.

I now felt much stronger about the eighteen-hour voyage ahead.

I was ready.

We all piled into the blue rubber inflatable boat, which looked like a slender letter 'U'. The bottom curve of the 'U' was the front of the boat, and the two arms, which we sat on, were like thick rubber pencils that were joined by a rubber floor.

The problem was, there were fifteen males and three females, and not enough space for all of us to sit. Yonas and I drew on our desert vehicle experience, and proceeded to sit all over each other!

There was a big difference between the sand and the water, though, particularly if anyone fell out. The desert was hard, but wouldn't swallow you. The sea was soft, but she'd eat you alive with her frigid, wave-serrated teeth. Needless to say, no one wanted to fall in.

As the boat headed into the sea's vast, open mouth, we sat still and solid. The further out we went, the more we stiffened. Every time water washed in, it slapped our faces with an icy hand, almost saying, 'Why take this risky journey? Are you crazy?'

No, we weren't crazy.

But we *were* desperate.

Persecution, violence, imprisonment, and war drove innocent people like us into the cold, watery arms of danger. Our reasons were never superficial or impulsive. They were for survival and betterment. Yes, our lives were at risk out at sea, but they were equally at risk on land.

Despite the dangers, the mood on the boat was relatively buoyant, at least to start with. All of us shared stories as we ate biscuits and sipped on water. Visualising land and a new life helped keep our spirits high.

All was going reasonably well until about sixteen hours in, when our sailor/guide had gone very quiet. His face looked as troubled as the water around us.

He turned to us with a lost expression.

Emphasis on the word *lost*.

'I'm sorry,' he apologised to the people near him. 'I've never used a compass and I think I misunderstood the boat seller's instructions in Libya. I normally navigate using the sun, moon, and stars. I don't know where we are.'

The bad news travelled to each person around the boat like a dreaded virus.

As each person caught it, their expression exposed the main symptom: fear.

No one became angry, though, including me. In the desert, I felt a combustion of rage when the vehicles broke down. Here, on the sea, the sailor was doing his best under difficult conditions. He simply made a mistake. We were all aware that staying calm meant staying alive. Instead of throwing accusations, we talked through ideas.

Eventually, the most sensible strategy prevailed: given we couldn't turn back (because we didn't know where *back* was), we decided we'd save petrol by turning off the engine. We'd then hover on the water until we saw another boat. When we saw another boat, we'd power the engine, race up, and ask for help.

It was a relatively simple plan that we implemented immediately.

Engine off.

Hover.

Watch.

No boats came.

We watched and waited.

No boats.

The hours passed.

No boats.

Our supplies dwindled.

No boats.

We got colder, hungrier, and thirstier.

Still, no boats.

My thoughts spiralled to bad places where dark questions lurked.

What was circling in the grey, choppy waters below?

How long could I hold my breath before breathing in water?

What did it feel like to have the sea gush into my lungs?

How long would it take to drown?

Just thinking these thoughts made me gasp for air.

Looking around, I could see others deep in thought too.

I watched my beautiful friend, Yonas.

Would our corpses float together or drift apart?

I realised that my life could end the same way it started: in danger. There was always danger, no matter where I was, or what

I did. Living in Eritrea. Leaving Eritrea. Staying in Sudan. Leaving Sudan. Staying in Libya. Leaving Libya.

Danger, always danger.

I often wondered when it would all end. Right now?

Just as I'd come to terms with my impending death for yet another time in my sixteen years of life, I heard a commotion from others on the boat.

People were pointing, sitting upright.

I looked at what they were pointing at.

A boat.

A boat?

A boat?!

A BIG BOAT!

It was the Italian Coastguard!

And a plane! There was a plane above!

Finally, our thirty-hour ordeal was over!

We were hollering and waving.

'HELLO!' I screamed up to the plane.

'HELP US!' someone else yelled at the coastguard boat nearby.

A person in the plane was filming us.

Although tired and weak, hilariously, some of the guys on the boat tidied their hair and started posing!

We all enjoyed an excited burst of energy.

I stopped thinking about death and started thinking about life.

I imagined drinking water again. Eating a meal. Wearing fresh, dry clothes. Standing on still, firm ground.

If not for the risk of capsizing, I would have jumped up and down with delight.

Yonas flung his arms around me in a relieved, jubilant hug. 'My flower,' he said, 'it's over, it's finally over! Our waiting and our dark troubles are over!'

But, were they?

We had been calling and waving, but nothing was happening.

After about thirty, long, confusing minutes, the plane just flew away.

Just like that. It flew away, off into the distance.

And the coastguard boat was pulling away too.

We began screaming. 'Wait! Don't leave us!'

The Eritrean sailor wasted no time putting our plan into action. He powered the engine and headed toward the coastguard's vessel, nudging our dinghy in front of them.

'Get out of the way!' one coastguard officer warned, waving for us to move.

Not a chance; we kept nudging in front of them.

They got frustrated.

We got frustrated.

But we refused to be left for dead.

Eventually, one person from our boat yelled, 'Please, just take the three girls on our boat.'

I was one of those three girls.

The coastguard officer yelled back, 'Only the three girls?'

'Yes! Only the three girls!'

He talked to someone else on his boat, then looked back at us. 'We'll take *only* the three girls. Do you understand? Only the three girls.'

'Yes, yes of course!'

We were allowed to position our U-shaped rubber boat next to theirs.

One of the Italian sailors leaned over to lift the first girl onto the boat, but it was tricky, so one of our guys offered to help by pushing her up.

He did this, but at the same time, he managed to climb on board himself, and then, began pulling others from our boat onto theirs. Pretty soon, everyone was helping everyone to clamber on! At first the coastguard crew tried to stop us, but eventually they relented.

It may seem like a dishonourable action from us, especially in light of the agreement, but it all happened quickly, spontaneously, and urgently. We were desperate, dehydrated, and starving. We were facing death on our own boat, or survival on theirs. Escaping was a knee-jerk reaction to preserve life. The coastguard captain knew this. If he forced all the males back onto the dinghy, they'd die. Could he live with this?

It seems not.

In fact, at the end of it all, not only did he let us onto the boat, he and his crew kindly gave us food and water.

We thanked them profusely. We smiled, ate, and drank, and for just a short while, could relax.

We enjoyed *the moment*, a warm bubble of time we rarely experienced.

Living amidst danger and persecution, it's unusual to surrender to the present because the past haunts you and the future taunts you. But just for *that* moment, we ate biscuits and drank juice, savouring the flavours as the breeze brushed our cheeks.

The captain took us to Lampedusa, a small island in southern Italy. There, we were given fresh clothes from a church group, and were placed in accommodations while the coastguard received orders from the authorities as to what to do with us.

After two days, they obtained their instructions, which were to take us to Sicily. So we all shuffled back onto the coastguard's boat, much drier and more hydrated than the last time.

In Sicily, everything moved quickly.

We were separated by gender.

We were asked questions.

We were put into a prison-like detention centre.

We were told we'd stay there for however long it took to process us.

The two other Eritrean girls and I stayed in a cell with a couple of women who spoke only Spanish and Italian. Even though we couldn't communicate with them, we co-habited just fine. That was fortunate, because we spent a *lot* of time in our cells. Days upon days, in fact. At least we were given one hour a week outside in a small, enclosed area. After breathing in stale air all week, the fresh air flowed through us like a purifying waterfall.

Twice, Yonas requested to see me, and we were given fifteen minutes with each other, fully supervised.

Apart from those highlights, though, the days were monotonous and dreary. Sometimes I'd talk to the Eritrean girls. Sometimes I'd pace. Sometimes I'd sleep. Sometimes I'd think.

The thinking was the worst. Having too much time alone with my thoughts was like running a race through a dense, dark forest.

The thoughts led to feelings: sadness, happiness, hope, anger, fear, longing, confusion.

Sometimes I experienced a dozen different emotions in a single minute, nearly every minute of the day. It was totally exhausting.

But eventually, after thirty days, we got some great news. We'd all been given temporary visas with permission to work in Italy!

At the same time as we were told the news, we were briefed on some important information. The government's preference was for us to stay in Sicily. In fact, we were offered 750 euros each to help us get on our feet, but it could only be withdrawn from the Bank of Sicily, *within* Sicily. We were able to withdraw 250 euros immediately, another 250 euros in a month, and the last 250 euros a month after that.

Shortly after hearing all this good news, we were released!

We hugged one another and rejoiced in the fact that we'd undertaken a perilous journey together, and survived. We shared a few war stories about the boat journey and our time in the detention centre, but mostly, we chatted excitedly about our plans.

My plan was to stay with a family friend in Naples before travelling to Germany to see my aunt. She was my mother's older sister who had sadly been receiving breast cancer treatment for the past eighteen months.

If not for my aunt, I probably would not have stayed in Italy. In Italy there were restrictions on schooling and further education, which meant I'd probably work as a cleaner indefinitely, just like many other Eritreans. Being a cleaner was honourable work; it just didn't provide the mental stimulation I needed, long-term.

As for the others, most were either staying with family and friends in Italy, or finding an Eritrean community in Sicily where they could seek information and temporary accommodations.

Yonas chose to stay in Sicily too. He knew one day he'd explore other opportunities and perhaps move to another country, but for now, he wanted to settle down. He thought I'd settle down with him. After all, even after I'd broken up with him in Libya, his hope was that we'd eventually get back together again when our circumstances improved. With a new beginning in Italy, he felt we could reignite the love we once shared.

How I wished! If there was *any* way I could have summoned those amorous feelings from Sudan, I would have done so in a heartbeat.

But I couldn't. I loved Yonas only as a friend. If I agreed to stay, I would be prolonging the pain, which was cruel. Better to surrender to the immediate uneasiness than to be a prisoner to later, mutual resentment.

So I told Yonas I was leaving for Naples, then Germany.

His face fell, as did my heart.

He tried to persuade me, cajole me, woo me. To no avail.

He deserved someone who adored him—no less.

When I hugged Yonas goodbye, his kindness left an imprint on my heart. I knew I would carry that imprint, always.

Indeed, I carried it all the way to Naples, then to Germany, where my aunt welcomed me with open arms.

Seeing my aunt ignited a flurry of mixed emotions.

In her eyes, I saw my mother.

In her body, I saw a cruel disease that robbed her of hair and weight.

But it didn't steal her vibrant smile.

I held her close. We talked for hours and hours, catching up on anything and everything.

My aunt invited me to stay with her for as long as I wanted. This was a generous offer, one I happily and gratefully accepted.

After spending a few days in Germany, however, I learned some unsettling news. I heard stories of refugees who had set up their lives in Germany, only to be deported after ten years, once their applications had been processed.

My excitement crumbled.

The thought of being deported to Eritrea at *any* time filled me with a cold, dark dread.

I was back to the same situation as Sudan. Back to living under a cloud of uncertainty. Back to being unable to fully settle: physically, emotionally, and psychologically.

My aunt and other relatives agreed it was a bad situation.

This meant I would need to be on the move again.

This meant I would need to make alternative plans, again.

I began researching nearby countries where the government was sympathetic to refugees. After reading a lot of information and making several calls, I learned that Belgium was a welcoming country, and fortunately was only approximately a six-hour drive away.

When I told my aunt, she was happy I'd found a more permanent alternative, though sad that I'd be leaving.

I arranged for a female and male acquaintance, Faven and Mohammed, to drive me to Belgium in exchange for petrol money. Eritreans will do almost anything for other Eritreans, even driving them to a nearby country!

As I waved goodbye to my aunt from the car, I was relieved to be embarking on a journey that wasn't death defying for a change. I sat in a bubble of gratitude for the entire drive, and after several hours, we pulled up at Robel's place.

Robel was a thirty-four-year-old Eritrean guy with whom I'd made arrangements, and who I'd vetted carefully while in Germany. He was happy to have me stay at his home for as long as I needed. Most Eritreans will help you, expecting little or nothing in return, because they've trudged along the same hard roads, and will do anything to make your path easier.

As we got out of the car, Robel strode toward us. It was around 8:00 p.m., and he was full of life. 'Welcome! Come in, come in! Nice to meet you in person, Fiori!'

'You too!'

'Thank you for the offer to come inside,' Faven said, 'but we won't stay long because we're driving back to Germany tonight.'

'Oh, but you *must* have a drink. My best friend is Awet. He doesn't live far. We can go to his home now.'

Typical Eritrean hospitality! Everyone loves a chance to catch up, no matter what the time, no matter what the relationship, no matter what the place.

Despite being tired, we still wanted to be sociable, so we all eagerly walked to his best friend's house, which was just around the corner.

Awet was as friendly and welcoming as Robel. Within moments, the laughter, conversation, food, and drink flowed. It's as though we were long lost friends.

Before we knew it, it was three o'clock in the morning, and we were all full and relaxed.

Not wanting us to leave while we were so tired, Awet invited us to stay in his one-bedroom unit. We agreed that it was the best course of action, and thanked him for the kind offer.

Even though Awet's home was tiny, we made it work. The three men slept side by side on mattresses on the lounge room floor, while Faven and I slept in the bed. Sleeping on the floor is quite a typical Eritrean tradition. No one thinks anything of it, nor do they mind sleeping right next to a stranger. We are all connected by a cultural umbilical cord that ties and binds us. We are all children of the same mother: Eritrea.

We fell asleep quickly, and woke up in a haze of groggy contentment the next morning.

As our brains kicked into gear, so did our mouths. It's as though someone had just pressed the 'pause' button on our conversation.

But we were also hungry! There wasn't much food at Awet's home, so Mohammed said he'd buy all of us breakfast, saying it was the least he could do after the warm hospitality from Awet and Robel.

Breakfast was a joyous continuation of the night before, with nice food, great company and lively discussions.

When we got back to Awet's home, we bid farewell to Faven and Mohammed, who both said they felt reassured that I had two trustworthy and caring friends in Belgium.

I agreed.

And I felt a fluttering deep in my belly.

It wasn't nerves.

It wasn't excitement.

It was an unfurling of the eagle's wings, again.

Fiori in Khartoum, where
she first met Yonas.

Fiori's brother, Amanuel.

Yonas, lying on the left, and Fiori, second
from right, with friends in Sudan.

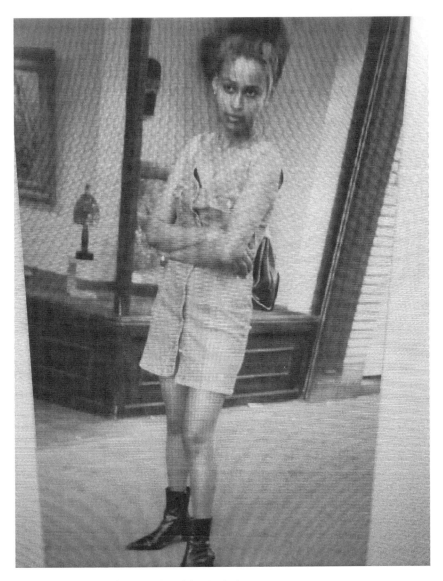

Fiori when she first arrived in Belgium.

Graduation day as a Certified Business and Executive Coach with the Life Coaching Institute in Australia in 2011.

Fiori stands proudly in her own office space in Melbourne, after establishing Transformations Coaching Group in 2011.

Fiori in the centre, while visiting friends in
Belgium in 2015: Awet (left) and Tim (second
from right) with two of her close girlfriends.

Fiori's brother Amanuel's girlfriend was six weeks pregnant when his boat went missing. His daughter lives in Sweden with her mother. Fiori (left) with her niece, while visiting in 2015.

Fiori (centre) took her parents to Israel in 2016 so they could
see the birthplace of Jesus, which was very important to them.

Fiori with her mother on holiday.

Fiori with her sister after 13 years apart.

This was a time when Fiori began coaching herself because she was unhappy and unfulfilled, even though her career in Australia was on track.

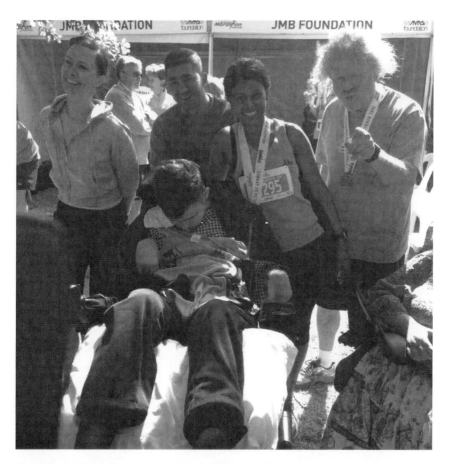

Fiori, in 2015, after running a half marathon to support the JMB Foundation, set up for James Macready-Bryan (seated, with his carers). James sustained an acquired brain injury after being senselessly assaulted on his twentieth birthday.

In 2015, Fiori expanded her business and was flourishing again.

Fiori and her life partner, Ben, with their son Odis, in 2018.

In my first week living with Robel, I put the wheels in motion to seek asylum in beautiful Belgium, which meant I needed to stay in a refugee detention centre. It was sad saying goodbye to Awet and Robel, especially knowing they'd be in Brussels, which was two hours away.

The detention centre was more spacious and open than the one in Italy, and although I was detained, I was certainly given more freedoms.

Regardless, being there was a huge cultural adjustment. All of a sudden I was eating cornflakes, which at the time tasted like bits of baked paper dipped in milk. Then, there was toast, which was a different size and flavour, but also from the cardboard family.

My stomach would grumble all day because I couldn't stomach the food, but I didn't let hunger hold me back. While I waited for my application to be processed, I poured all my time and energy into learning Dutch.

Learning the language was the key to my assimilation and finding work, if and when I received a temporary visa.

It was always on my mind that I had to find work, fast. I was tired of being away from Amanuel.

Belgium is the place where I'd settle, the safe haven to which I would bring Amanuel. I wasn't sure exactly how I'd bring him, but I knew it would require a lot of money. So I had to start earning. (I knew Mum and Dad would help too, but the Eritrean Nafka would convert to very little.)

With that goal always front and centre in my mind, I studied furiously.

In the morning, when I was too tired to even eat breakfast, I'd study.

In the middle of the day, when I was going stir-crazy, I'd study.

At night, when I dreamt of breathing in fresh air under glittery skies, I'd study.

But studying was hard because I was distracted by the uncertainty of my situation, which was highlighted to me every time I had a visa application interview. There was so much pressure during these interviews because if the person thought I was lying, he or she would deport me back to Eritrea immediately.

But here's the problem.

In my culture, and due to the way I was raised, I was taught it was disrespectful to look directly into older people's eyes or the eyes of those in authority. Yet, if I looked down during the interview, it suggested I was being dishonest or had something to hide.

I had to adapt. I had to defy my upbringing in order to defy my destiny.

Adding to the distractions at the detention centre, I wasn't allowed to have my own space. The restrictions felt almost toxic at times, robbing me of oxygen, draining me of energy, affecting my ability to concentrate. The restrictions even blurred my mental image of Amanuel, which I needed to keep crisp and clear at all times.

Mercifully, I was allowed a few local calls weekly where I'd usually speak to Robel and Awet. Both were my lifeline to the outside world. When I spoke to them, I pictured their small homes filled with love and warmth. I longed to feel toasty and cosy in their cocoons of fun and friendship.

My floundering attitude must have been noticeable and worrying, because Robel made some enquiries. He discovered that if he signed papers to acknowledge he was responsible for me, I could be released into his care.

When he told me the news, I was practically dancing on the spot. 'Thank you!' I squealed. 'How soon can you come and sign the papers?!'

He came as fast as he could, and I was out. After two months in the detention centre, I was back in Brussels, in the little unit with a big heart.

As always, there was no time to waste.

I enrolled immediately in a language school and threw myself into everyday activities to practise communicating with Dutch speakers.

Just like my Arabic-learning days, I surrendered my pride to talk to as many people as possible. Sometimes I felt like I was tangled in a sticky, thick web of words and sentences. But I always managed to claw my way out.

Integration was a priority.

I owed Belgium everything. She, and the majority of her people, were incredibly kind to me.

Belgium gave me something I had never experienced before—a life without feeling constantly fearful.

I felt like someone had removed heavy shackles from my feet.

I felt like nothing could stop me now.

Hope was everywhere. Appreciation swelled in my heart daily. Every moment, I was eternally grateful that Belgium's system was willing to help a complete stranger like me—to help me settle, to learn the language, to study, and one day, possibly have full citizenship. Belgium embraced the fundamental core of our existence: that we should help others, especially the vulnerable and voiceless.

I vowed I would do everything to contribute to Belgium's economy when given the opportunity, which included moving to Antwerp, a different Belgium city where there were more jobs.

And wonderfully, that opportunity came within five months, when I got my temporary work visa.

It was time to head to Antwerp.

It was time to better myself, enable myself to better Amanuel's life, and contribute to Belgium's prosperity.

Antwerp, like Brussels, was a city dotted with exquisite architecture and lined with quaint, cobbled lanes. As beautiful as it was, though, there was little time for leisurely sightseeing.

It was down to business.

I found a place to rent.

I started looking for work.

I enrolled in language classes.

Actually, rather than taking one language class a day, I enrolled in three. That might seem extreme, but I would have taken more if it was possible. I needed to become semi-fluent, super-fast. The better my language, the better-paying jobs I'd get. In the meantime, though, I'd do what I'd always done when first arriving in a new city. I'd look for cleaning or kitchenhand work, which paid less, but was easy to get.

However, these jobs *weren't* easy to get in Belgium.

When employers asked where I was from, and I replied 'Africa,' they'd either hang up in my ear or tell me the job was filled. This was a shock. Not getting work was foreign to me, and yet, it was *because* I was foreign that I wasn't getting work.

My attitude could have gone one of two ways. I could have felt vilified and horrified, painting all Belgians with one, angry brush. Or, I could feel empathy.

I chose empathy, because it was the happier, healthier choice. It helped me, rather than hurt me. It equipped me to define my destiny rather than divert or destroy it.

I was a black girl in a predominantly white society, so I was able to step out of my skin to see people's fear. The employers discriminated against me because of what they'd experienced, or what they thought *might* happen.

I was still hurt by the racism, of course, but I knew their beliefs didn't represent the beliefs of everyone. As such, I definitely didn't stereotype the entire country based on the actions of a few, because that's what was being done to me.

I realised that if I wanted to get work, I had to change with the new circumstances. I had to adapt.

I decided that in Antwerp I would *not* actively seek out other Eritreans to spend all my time with, as I'd done in nearly every other city.

Yes, there was great comfort and joy relating to people from my own country, especially when I sometimes felt alone, misunderstood, and discriminated against. But the only way to change incorrect perceptions was to organically let my honesty and integrity shine through, particularly around the people who owned those perceptions.

I ignored any discrimination and focused on my own truth, and the genuine, wholesome truths of those around me. I headed out onto the streets, I got involved with groups, and I made many wonderful friends.

Looking for work was no longer a chore. Before each call I'd say, 'I deserve this job. I'm good enough.'

If the person hung up in my ear, or told me the position was filled, I'd say to myself, 'Focus on the next call. Get the next job.'

The change in mindset was small, and yet absolutely enormous. It must have created subtle, noticeable differences in my tone and answers, because not only did I get *a* job, I got a *few* jobs, all of them working around my three daily language classes.

The curse had gone, and my usual optimism returned.

My busy life returned too!

I attended language classes Monday through Thursday of each week from 9:00 a.m. until 12:30 p.m., then 1:00 p.m. to 4:00 p.m., and finally from 6:30 p.m. to 10:00 p.m. On Fridays I worked as a cleaner for a single mother of three. On Saturdays, I cleaned an office from 7:00 a.m. to 9:00 a.m., and as soon as that shift ended, I dashed to a Spanish restaurant nearby to wash dishes from 9:00 a.m. to 11:00 p.m. On Sundays, I worked at the same Spanish restaurant from 9:00 a.m. to 10:00 p.m.

Phew!

The restaurant shifts were the hardest because I spent the entire time on my feet. On Monday morning I'd limp to language classes, my legs feeling like two wobbly pillars of aching, throbbing mush.

I could barely stand, let alone walk.

So, I did what I've always done.

I put one foot in front of the other.

By Wednesday my legs would feel slightly better.

On Thursday and Friday, I'd be back to normal.

And by the weekend, it would start all over again!

Although my routine was busy and physically exhausting, I always made time to call Amanuel. My goal of bringing him to Belgium was like a jewel, burning in the middle of my heart, keeping me centred.

Sometimes, when I thought my legs would collapse just three hours into a shift, an image of Amanuel would pop into my head, and I'd keep standing. I'd move painfully from one foot to the other for the rest of the day, thinking of him.

I wouldn't give up.

I *couldn't* give up.

It helped that I still spent a lot of my time being involved with Belgium's culture, and spending time with positive, amazing people.

One of those people was William, a Belgian man I met at a foreigner integration meeting.

William was an older gentleman who took me under his wing. He kindly introduced me to his wife and children, and he became like a father to me. He invited me to spend holidays with his family so I wouldn't feel alone or isolated, and even taught me how to drive a car. With people like William in the world, there was goodness and hope.

Two other incredible people I met at different times became my boyfriends! One lovely guy was Alexander, and another was a journalist named Tim.

Tim probably embodies the tolerance, love, and acceptance of many Belgians. He was an intelligent, well-respected political journalist who would get stopped on the street by fans. I was a foreigner who washed dishes and who didn't speak Dutch very well; yet, he looked past my occupation and fluency, to see *me*.

On the odd days when the discrimination or racism was too much, Tim would wrap me in his wings of tolerance and love. He assured me that I was worthy. That I was enough. These were things I knew, but needed to hear during melancholy moments. On the days when my shifts were long and my whole body ached, he told me that my drive, diligence, and work ethic would ensure such jobs were only temporary. To receive reassurance and acknowledgement from someone so esteemed, who could be with anyone, but who chose to be with me, was beyond uplifting and heartening.

Even after we stopped being boyfriend and girlfriend, Tim and I remained friends, just as you'd expect of two people who respected each other.

Work-wise, I eventually started applying for positions that required a higher level of Dutch and a lower level of physical pain. And I got a job!

Where?

McDonald's!

When the McDonald's manager shook my hand after the successful interview, memories of every late night studying Dutch, every awkward conversation, every class I'd taken, filled my mind. I felt as though I'd reached an important marker during a gruelling marathon. Getting the job was like an encouraging round of applause.

I smiled at those golden arches each day, walking through the doors with a determined, spring in my step.

One of the biggest benefits of working at McDonald's was the level of customer interaction, which meant my Dutch improved swiftly and consistently. So much so, in fact, that my language teacher gave me the green light to start studying business administration. This was music to my ears, because my *ultimate* goal was to get a job in an office, where the work was mentally challenging and paid better. I wasted no time enrolling in both an administration course and a computer course, around my work shifts at McDonald's.

The moment I started the courses, it was like returning home. I'd never formally studied business in my life, and yet, it was like walking into a room that I'd set up long ago, where the furniture was worn but loved. Everything about business felt natural and right, so even before finishing the courses, I landed a part-time administration role for a market research company. When I got that position, an energy soared through my body that I'd never experienced before—an energy that lifted my spirits so high, I could almost touch the hands of my grandmothers and great-grandmothers.

After a while, I also applied for jobs based overseas. The thought of climbing up the administration ladder while also discovering new cities and frontiers was exciting. In many cases, the actual job interviews were overseas as well, rather than in Belgium. In one instance, I was flown to China by a boat-building company. On another occasion I was flown to India by a sugar company.

As with all jobs, I found out more about the positions as I progressed through the recruitment process. Even though I was humbled to be offered the roles, unfortunately there were aspects of each I didn't feel comfortable with. Regardless, I was thrilled to be considered for the jobs in the first place, let alone be offered them!

My destiny was constantly being defied, not by chance, but by choice. Not by any stroke of luck, but by blood, sweat, and tears. And it was happening because of small, everyday decisions, rather than singular, earth-moving actions.

If I had stayed in Eritrea and surrendered to my destiny, I would likely have been killed during the war or given a personal death sentence of being a child bride and mother. My dreams would have been buried under a tribe of children, my ambitions knocked out of me, perhaps *literally* by my husband.

I had crossed countries and cities to escape both danger and destiny.

Now I was in Belgium, my wings colourful and strong.

Even when I was able to give up my Dutch language classes, I continued studying. I completed the courses of director secretariat, basic accounting, and business management. Some of these courses were online, but I'd travel to Brussels to complete the exams, giving me a wonderful opportunity to catch up with friends like Awet and Robel.

I loved meeting my dear friends, making new friends, and contributing to Belgium.

Life was wonderful.

But, I missed Amanuel.

Terribly.

Every breath I took was for him, to oxygenate our plans to one day be together.

He was the jewel within my heart.

The life force that held me together.

Holding him, hugging him, seeing him, was all tantalisingly within reach.

However, was the beautiful Belgium I knew and loved actually safe enough? Because just around the corner, blood would stain the cobbled streets, and put fear into the hearts of tolerant, loving people.

CHAPTER SIX

HEAVEN AND HELL

---

*Pain must be experienced. To distract from
it, or to dull it, simply strengthens its resolve
and its cold, dark hold on your soul.*

I t was a clear day in May when an eighteen-year-old man walked through central Antwerp.

The city's streets fanned out around him, inviting him to walk a path, to choose a destiny.

The trams snaked to interesting, uplifting destinations, tempting him to jump on.

The pointed tops of narrow, clustered buildings showed him the sky, and how far up he could fly.

The man looked down though.

Deep down, into the heart of darkness.

He opened his bag.

He pulled out a cold hunter's rifle.

He looked up again, and calmly targeted foreigners to shoot and kill.

He saw a Turkish woman.

He fired. She was seriously injured.

He saw a black woman.

He shot her. She fell, dead.

In the black woman's care was a two-year-old native Flemish girl, also killed. A casualty of his racism.

The police arrived quickly, shooting him in the stomach. He was taken to hospital where he survived. He was later charged for the crimes.

When I heard about the tragedy, I felt crushed.

Bullets rained down on Eritrea often. Bodies were blown. Blood splattered walls. Screams sliced the sky.

It was a horrifying kind of normal. Revolting, but not rare.

Here in Belgium, though, a corpse on cobblestones seemed gruesomely out of place.

True, there had been racially-motivated incidents in the past, but this was the worst.

The incident shook many to the core, as it did me.

Death had stained the streets; the marks would blemish forever.

All of a sudden, I asked myself questions I'd never asked before.

What if Amanuel had been in the firing line? What if *his* life was in danger in Belgium?

I could never live with myself if I promised him freedom, only to deliver death.

As it turns out, I needn't have worried. Weeks later, tens of thousands of people marched in Antwerp to protest against the murders, and the vitriolic racism that fuelled them.

The protest was silent, proving that no words can speak louder and more effectively than the longest sentences. The government listened because the silence was ear-splitting. It boomed from hearts and it bellowed from minds.

Although there were still many racist people in Belgium, overall, the season was changing. There was a positive shift. A movement. A growing.

Posters in the windows read, '*Zonder haat straat*,' meaning 'Streets without hate.'

People were speaking up and speaking out.

That's the beauty of democracy. You can share your views without being killed, tortured, or imprisoned.

In Belgium, the people were reviled, so they rallied. They demanded change, and they got it.

The country had been brought to its knees. But the people stood up, as one, for what was right.

I was no longer afraid for Amanuel. These were the streets, *the streets without hate*, on which I felt comfortable for my brother to walk.

As the years went by, I put firmer steps in place to bring Amanuel to Belgium, to these streets without hate. As well as working in administration, I worked a number of different jobs on the side to save enough money.

I missed Amanuel's tight black curls; his big, wondrous eyes; and his straight brown nose.

Over time, he'd turned from a boy into a man. I had missed the transformation, and I didn't want to miss any more changes.

Joyfully, we were making progress.

Amanuel had escaped the dangers of Eritrea in much the same way I had. He travelled through Sudan and was now in transit in Libya.

However, he was stuck because of an understandable fear of crossing the sea.

He was in danger if he left, but he was also in danger if he stayed.

'Libya is unkind to me, Fiori,' Amanuel would say over the phone. 'The people are so cruel.'

I'd nod empathetically but respond matter-of-factly. 'When you were in Sudan, I told you not to travel to Libya because I knew the challenges you'd face. I wanted to find another way, but you insisted on going. Now you're in Libya; we just have to work on a solution. I've sent you money. I've told you what to do. Please, get on a boat and come over.'

'Fiori, remember when we lived together in elementary school?' he'd digress. 'I really love you so much. I miss you so much.'

He was a master at changing the topic!

'I love you and miss you too, Amanuel,' I'd say. 'That's why I want you here with me.'

'There's no rush, Fiori,' he'd soothe. 'Our ever-loving God will decide when the time is right. It will just happen. Let me investigate more.'

I'd dig my fingernails into the phone. 'No Amanuel, it won't just *happen*. You have to *make* it happen. How many times have you been thrown in prison, beaten up, and had our money stolen or scammed from you? How many times have you been spat on when walking down the street? You're in danger there. It's time to make a move.'

'The boat ride is risky. Look what happened to you.'

'Yes, it's risky, but so is living in Libya. If you're reluctant to take the boat journey, that's okay. Head back to Sudan, and we'll find another way.'

'No, the desert journey was long and dangerous. I can't go back to Sudan.'

'Then you're stuck, Amanuel. You've trapped yourself.'

'Maybe, but remember as kids when we …'

And on he'd go, reminiscing about beautiful times from a past that was slipping from his grasp.

Each week our conversations became more and more strained. I was convinced he'd remain wedged between the desert and the sea forever.

But one day, after a long two years in Libya, surprisingly he called me out of the blue.

'Fiori, a group of us have organised a boat.'

I almost fell off my chair, but I was guarded. 'Don't joke around Amanuel. Is this real? Is this actually happening?'

'It's really happening. We'll be together soon.'

'That's wonderful news, Amanuel! What are the details?'

'It's a big boat, so the journey should take about three days. We'll also be staying in a secret house until we're clear to leave, so don't worry too quickly. I'll contact you as soon as I can. In the meantime, please pray for me.'

'Of course I'll pray for you! But you will be fine. This is goodbye, only for now.'

And with that, I bid him farewell.

My brother had started his journey! It took years of cajoling and convincing while he suffered in Libya, but finally he was on his way to freedom.

I grabbed a photo of Amanuel and held it to my chest.

I held it there all day.

And the next day.

And the next day too.

Four days later I was still holding it, more tightly than usual.

Time was ticking.

I'd completed the journey, so I knew there could be delays.

When a call finally came through on my mobile phone, I jumped with fright.

I hoped it was Amanuel calling from the satellite phone on the boat, which I knew could only make calls, not receive them.

'Hello? Amanuel?'

At first I couldn't hear very well because the line was crackly.

'Fiori, help!' he pleaded.

I couldn't breathe. My heart seemed to stop working.

'Our boat engine has broken,' he said. 'The boat is taking on water. Please arrange for help quickly!'

My mouth was open but no words came out.

'Fiori, are you there?!' he yelled.

I snapped back to reality.

'I'm here! Yes, I'm here. Listen to me. Listen carefully. Find out your coordinates from the sailor.'

I heard muffles. He came back to the phone and told me.

'Okay good,' I said, scribbling down the coordinates. 'I'll get you help. Stay calm. I'm on it!'

When I got off the call, my entire body was trembling. My breathing was fast. My fingers were tingling.

I had to slow everything down. I had to be calm.

As much as I could, I focused on the moment.

I tried to stop thinking of what had led to the event.

I tried to stop thinking about what could happen.

I tried to focus only on what I could do right now.

I dashed to my computer.

I looked up numbers.

I called everyone I could think of: Italian border security, Italian police, humanitarian organisations, The United Nations. I also called the Maltese police, because they were naturally closer to Malta than Italy. But everyone I spoke to seemed dismissive or disinterested. They kept referring me to other agencies and organisations.

I felt hopeless and helpless.

I paced the room.

I clutched the phone to my body.

I felt like my brain was about to blow out of my head.

Then the phone rang.

I answered it fast. 'Hello?! Hello?!'

Amanuel's voice was quick and quavering: 'Have you sent someone?'

I wanted to burst into tears. I wanted to cry a river that would wash me right to my brother, so I could hug him and hold him and swim him safely back to Belgium. But I kept my voice strong and solid. 'Yes, I've made many calls, Amanuel. Sit tight, and someone will come soon. Call me when they do. Keep staying in touch. I'm going to make more calls.'

I called everyone I'd previously spoken to, several times. I begged them to *please* help.

I held the photo of Amanuel close to my chest. I started praying because it was the only thing I *could* do.

I prayed like I'd never prayed before.

'God, you *know* Amanuel. He is soft, gentle, and kind. *Please* deliver him safely to me. Please keep his boat afloat.'

I prayed all day.

I had to.

If I didn't pray, my mind wandered to the deep, dark depths of a merciless ocean. To the clawing paws of lapping water. To the capsizing of vessels and the floundering of arms. To gasps and screams. To thunderous silence.

Where there was prayer, there was concentration and comfort, not catastrophes.

But staying focused was a battle.

After a few hours, I made all the calls again.

And again.

Eventually, I got some news.

'A Maltese Airforce plane has seen the boat,' said a man from one of the agencies.

I gasped. 'Are you sure?'

'Yes, they took a photo. It's adrift around 150 kilometres south of Malta. There are around fifty passengers on board.'

'Will they be rescued?'

He went quiet. 'You'll need to wait for further information.'

I knew what that meant. As I hung up the phone, I wanted to crush it. While I was relieved the boat had been spotted, I had a hunch they'd simply taken a photo and flown away.

I was crying, panicking, stressing, and praying.

Later, somewhere in the blurry hours of misery and exhaustion, I checked the news on my computer.

The story of my brother's boat had been picked up by the media. There was even a photo. My heart clamoured against my rib cage as my eyeballs flitted over the clump of colour to see if I could find Amanuel.

Where was he?

I *needed* to see him.

The faces weren't recognisable. The grainy photo was taken from too far away. However, I *could* see their body language, and they seemed relaxed—which made sense because they probably thought they were about to be saved. I had been in the same situation, looking up from our adrift vessel to the plane above, thanking God that we were about to be rescued, only to see the plane abandon us.

From the article, it appeared that other family members had been making calls, just as I'd been doing. I also read that the UNHCR (United Nations High Commissioner for Refugees) asked the coastguard and Maltese government why they didn't save the people on the boat. The answer? The conditions were too dangerous to pursue a rescue.

The photo told another story. It told a story of calm waters. Anyone who looked at the photo would see how calm the sea was, and as it turned out, over the coming hours many people *would* look at the photo, and many people *would* demand answers.

The coastguard was eventually ordered to send a search boat out to find my brother's vessel.

Halleluiah!

Better late than never?

No. As it turns out, late may have been too late.

After my brother's boat had been right under their noses, now they couldn't find it. They scanned the waters for days.

After five consecutive days, the search was called off.

That was it. That was the end of any practical assistance I could offer my brother, who for all I knew, was still counting on me to rescue him. When I heard the news, I curled up in a ball on the floor.

I wished the earth's core would devour me.

Was this really happening?

This *couldn't* be happening.

Amanuel was still out there.

Why weren't they continuing their search?

He could be alive, washed up on a shore, or clinging to a piece of debris.

Was he crying?

Was he shaking?

Was he hopeful?

Was he still waiting for me, his protector?

Thoughts and images poured into my mind like water into a sinking boat.

And eventually, my mind sunk.

It sunk to the depths of hell.

A misery so great took hold of me.

My tears fell into the carpet.

My sobs shook the earth.

I spent hours on the ground, shaking and crying.

I wept violently. I drowned in my own tears. I sank to the bottom of an ocean of sadness.

Down there, lying on the sandy bottom of sorrow, I thought of my parents.

They didn't know the search had been called off yet, that their son was missing.

I had to tell them.

I scrubbed my eyes with my arm sleeve, took a deep breath, and slowly got to my knees.

From there, I summoned all my will to stand on my feet.

I then got my phone, sat on the lounge, and prepared to make the hardest call of my life.

I'd kept in touch with my parents throughout the ordeal. They were waiting expectantly for good news. I anticipated Mum's wails when I told them, which made it difficult to dial the number. At least my dad was out of jail. He could support Mum even though his own pain would be great.

I dialled. They picked up the phone.

There's no easy way to speak the unspeakable, so I just said it. 'The search has been called off. No sign of the boat or Amanuel.'

There was silence at first, then an onslaught of tears.

Wails.

Questions.

Anger.

Their divine boy was missing. A life Mum had carried. A man Dad had moulded.

A black cloud seemed to stretch from Belgium to my parents' home in Eritrea, uniting us in grief.

We huddled under it. Far apart, but side-by-side.

When the call eventually ended, my head thumped from all the crying.

I lay on the couch in the foetal position.

Random images of my brother popped into my mind.

Images of him as a baby, a boy, a man.

What had I done?

Was this my fault?

He wasn't ready to travel.

I kept pushing him and pushing him.

I sent him to the sea.

I refused to believe he'd drowned. I refused!

The coastguard hadn't spotted them.

Maybe he'd been rescued by another boat?

Perhaps they were on an island somewhere?

There was still hope, no matter how thin and frail it was.

He was missing. *Not* dead.

But I was.

I was nothing more than a lifeless shell.

I couldn't go to work the next week. I couldn't face happy people on the streets, in offices, on public transport. I couldn't smile or interact. In fact, when I saw others, I'd ask myself, 'How can they continue to exist normally when everything in the world is off balance?'

I stayed at home instead.

Each moment, I sunk into sad scenarios.

I slumped over broken dreams.

I slid into misery.

Day after day, I'd wake up with a grief hangover.

My head pulsated from constant sobs.

My sagging eyes were shadowed by half-moons.

I didn't care.

I allowed myself to feel what I needed to feel.

I didn't dull it, ignore it, suppress it, or deny it.

I cocooned myself in misery and memories.

I knew one day I'd crawl out.

That 'one day' didn't come for at least a few weeks, but I did crawl out eventually.

Slowly, organically, gently, painfully.

I tentatively returned to the world and to my jobs, but it was in a dream-like state. Everything around me seemed to move in slow motion.

I put on a neutral mask during the day, and ripped it off at night.

My apartment was both my sanctuary and my cell.

It was a place where I could be alone and real, yet, it was also a place where I was locked in a vault of memories.

Amanuel was everywhere. This little apartment was going to be our home. For years I'd imagined him sitting at the table, cooking in the kitchen or lounging on the couch. Those ghostly imprints of him were everywhere.

For months, I simply existed. I completed tasks mechanically during the day, and fell into an exhausted, emotional heap at night.

Sometimes the pain was so overwhelming I thought it would kill me.

In fact, one night I was convinced I *would* die.

I was convinced my heart, heavy with sadness, would eventually slow to one, final thump.

I was so convinced that I called my dear friend, Awet, to notify him. We had talked many times over the past few months, and he always provided a kind, listening ear. Today though, I needed to give him clear instructions. I needed to get down to business. 'Awet, do you love me?'

He was taken aback by my bluntness.

'Of course I do. Why?'

'I want you to love me enough not to fight me on something. I want you to love me enough not to argue with me. I want you to do something, and I don't want you to question or challenge me. Okay?'

'Fiori, you're scaring me. What do you want me to do?'

'You first have to promise that you will do as I ask.'

'Okay, okay, I promise. What is it?'

'Remember Awet, you promised, okay?'

'Okay!'

I spoke slowly but clearly. 'I have a feeling that tonight I'm going to die in my sleep.'

'Fiori!'

'It's okay,' I said. 'I probably won't. But if I haven't contacted you in two days, please call the police in Antwerp so they can find my body. I don't want my apartment to smell.'

'Fiori ...'

'Awet, please don't try to convince me otherwise, just stick to your promise and do what I've asked. If you truly love me, you'll do as you promised.'

'I'm coming over ...'

'AWET!'

'I'll take the metro. Wait for me. Don't go to sleep. Don't do anything.'

He then hung up.

'Awet? AWET!'

I hung up the phone and angrily threw it on my bed. I wanted to scream. Why didn't he just listen? He promised! I instantly regretted calling him.

My phone rang, and I assumed it was Awet, *hopefully* calling to apologise. *Hopefully* telling me he wasn't coming over.

'Hello!' I barked.

The voice on the other end was soft, reluctant almost. 'Fiori? It's Alexander.'

Alexander was my ex-boyfriend, with whom I had remained friends. Why was *he* calling? I cleared my throat and said, 'Alexander, this is not a good time. I'll call you tomorrow. I've got to go.'

'Fiori, *please* don't hang up. I have to talk to you.'

'Fine, what is it? What is the urgent matter that can't wait till tomorrow?'

'I can't stop thinking about you. I know you've been dealing with your grief, but I feel that something isn't right with you tonight. Can I please come and see you, even just for a minute? I just want to see that you're okay, then I'll leave.'

How on earth did he know I was possibly going to die tonight?

'Fiori ...'

'No!' I blurted. 'Don't come. I'm busy. Now is just not a good time. Sorry, I've got to go.'

I hung up, shaking.

How did he know?

Alexander called again.

'I'm coming, Fiori. I can tell there's definitely something wrong. I can't rest until I see you, until I know you're okay.'

'I'm telling you, I'm fine. I'm just busy. Now just isn't a good time. Can you visit next week?'

'No, I need to visit now.'

'Well you can't,' I snapped.

I hung up, and I *wasn't* picking up the phone again.

My head was in a spin. Awet was coming, and now possibly Alexander? This is *not* how I thought the night would be. I thought I'd put my head down to sleep and never wake again. I thought I'd never have to claw through the thick mass of misery and memories ever again. Never walk through the throbbing, continual ache that had become my life.

Instead, within a couple of hours, two kind-hearted men—Awet and Alexander—were sitting by my side.

They had come because they couldn't and wouldn't let a friend suffer alone.

I relinquished my need for solitude.

I allowed myself to cry.

I surrendered myself to their compassion. In doing so, the pain in my heart broke through my skin in the form of a feverish sweat.

I lay down, and each of them took turns dabbing my head with a wet towel.

They watched over me.

They said nothing, yet their actions spoke volumes.

They were like guardian angels, being with me as I lay in hell, but never letting the flames completely engulf me.

They didn't rescue or distract.

They let me lie in my hurt; they let me sweat in my sadness.

They knew, like me, that pain has a pathway. To distract from it, or to dull it, simply strengthens its resolve and its cold, dark hold on your soul. The only way to let it pass through is to be courageous enough to first let it in.

I eventually fell asleep, waking in the morning to see both of them sleeping, one in a chair near me, the other on the couch.

During the darkest night of my life, when I thought I would shrivel into my burning sorrow, I woke up to fight another day.

Because of my two beautiful friends.

———————>●<———————

My headspace had improved marginally after that sad, difficult night. I had thanked Awet and Alexander profusely, and had kept in touch with both.

But one problem remained.

Painful reminders of Amanuel were everywhere—in my apartment, around Antwerp, all over Belgium.

He appeared at the landmarks I would have taken him to, the places he may have worked, the spots he would have relaxed.

Consequently, there were many parts of Belgium I couldn't bear to look at anymore. They were constant reminders that Amanuel was missing—not that I needed any more reminding, because thoughts and memories plagued me daily.

Belgium was becoming like a tomb, filled with death and darkness.

It was a problem, and I had to focus on a solution.

I realised that in order to leave the reminders, I needed to disrupt their continual flow. I needed to leave Belgium, even just for a short time, to stem the cycle of sadness.

I had to go somewhere far away.

Somewhere untouched by plans or memories involving Amanuel.

That's when I thought of my friend, Angesom.

Angesom lived in Australia, a country about which I knew very little. Actually, all I knew was that it was quite far away; *so* far away it was practically 'down under', at the bottom of the world.

Perfect. The bottom of the world sounded far enough to me.

Amanuel was in many places, but he wasn't in Australia. Maybe I could visit Angesom?

I knew the trip wouldn't remove my grief, but it would temporarily remove the constant bombardment of external, painful reminders.

I called Angesom to propose a visit.

He was happy to hear from me, and during the conversation he said the words I was longing to hear, 'Yes Fiori, come to Australia!'

He understood my purpose, and he was excited for me. In different circumstances, I would have been excited too. For now, though, I was just relieved.

I thanked Angesom, telling him I'd set the wheels in motion as soon as possible.

And I did. Those wheels turned and churned. Within a month I got my visa and organised time off from my jobs. Before I knew it, I was sitting on a plane bound for Australia.

Planes are a hub of excitement, and although I could see other people's joy as they filed down the aisle looking for their seats, I couldn't experience joy myself.

It was painful being an onlooker rather than a participant, so I gazed out of the window instead.

I kept staring, even as the plane took off and the tarmac became nothing but a distant tick. Even as the country became nothing but a colourful pattern within a kaleidoscope.

I even kept looking as the ocean stretched out like an ivory-flecked, blue veil.

But there, the neutral emotions stopped, and an irrational panic set in.

I pressed my face against the window.

Amanuel?

Was he down there?

I strained to see him.

What's that, in the distance?

Could it be a boat?

'The wing hasn't fallen off, has it?' joked the man next to me.

His words snapped me back to reality, out of my illogical urgency.

I smiled. I shook my head.

I returned to my window-watching, this time calmly, looking for my tiny, sparkling star in a universe of water. Amanuel wasn't there, of course.

I welcomed the plane's climb into the clouds. It was peaceful up high, far from the water.

Floating amidst the clouds, I prayed for my beautiful brother who, to me, was still missing, not dead. I prayed that he was safe. That he forgave me. That his hair was dry and his eyes were wide. That he could carry on without me by his side.

Praying also gave me strength for the next chapter of my journey.

So, when the plane finally touched down in Melbourne, I felt capable and ready.

After alighting and collecting my bags, I saw Angesom.

He laughed and waved joyfully.

My smile came easily and naturally, not forced, for the first time in such a long while.

A small step, a tiny win.

We hugged, and after chatting briefly at the airport, we headed to his home in Fitzroy, continuing to talk the whole way.

Angesom pointed out various sites from the public transport. Melbourne reminded me of Belgium with its trams and bustling traffic, but thankfully, Amanuel didn't wave at me from every curb.

Another small step, another small win. I could already feel these small steps would lead to some sort of healing.

Angesom dropped me at his unit but needed to return to work. He told me to relax, help myself to food, and if I wanted to, explore the city.

The latter was most appealing. I thanked him, and I hit the streets.

I started exploring, and before I knew it, I found myself walking from his Fitzroy home right to the heart of Melbourne's CBD. I noticed a pureness and freshness about the country that seemed to flow through the veins of every person I met.

People smiled.

They said hello.

They struck up conversations. The Australian accent was relaxed and fun, like a heartfelt giggle carried in the breeze.

I found myself smiling a lot, which caused me to feel guilty.

How dare I feel joy!

Where was Amanuel?

Was *he* feeling joy?

What right do I have?

What sort of a horrible person am I?

My soul plummeted to the pavement, and it was there, sprawled on the cold concrete, that I realised I had to change my mindset. I told myself, 'Fiori, this has to stop. Otherwise, what's the point of the trip? You may as well be in Belgium, totally miserable.'

I decided I would acknowledge my guilt rather than retreat into it. See it, rather than surrender to it.

Then, let it go.

It was hard to do. *Very* hard. But as the days passed, I smiled more, and felt guilty less.

Over the course of my holiday, Angesom took me to visit amazing places and beautiful people. His Eritrean friends seemed to be everywhere. In fact, one day he took me to Crown Casino, and an Eritrean-Australian friend, Jakob, came over to say hello.

I found myself gazing up at Jakob's chiselled jaw, slicked back hair, and dark eyes.

Jakob had been in Australia a long time, and I would classify him more as an Aussie guy than an Eritrean one. His demeanor was laid back, and he seamlessly possessed equal measures of charm and ruggedness.

Being around Jakob seemed to unfreeze the numbness in my heart.

I could feel my heart *beat* again. Robustly, not robotically. Perhaps, even with a flutter?

When Jakob suggested we all go to a bar the next day, I was open to the idea.

I was open to it the next day as well, and the next day too.

Soon, Jakob started taking me out on his own. We went to restaurants, bars, landmarks, and beaches.

He held my hand sometimes, which felt right, and made me feel safe.

I loved the way he took charge. Protected me.

Conversation flowed easily too. Jakob told me about his family, his friends, his interests, his work. I was not surprised that he managed a team of twenty-five people in his position as a production planner. He had a cool but commanding air about him that made me assume he was in a leadership role.

I felt so comfortable with Jakob that I opened the book of my life to him, tentatively turning pages, and eventually explaining whole chapters.

I told him how much I hated violence and war. How much I loved family and friends, and how deeply I missed my beloved Amanuel.

Sitting open and vulnerable, we both found ourselves wanting more than just friendship.

Our occasional hand-holding turned into a permanent fixture. Our kisses on the cheek became kisses on the lips. Our brief hugs became long embraces.

Our friendship became romantic, and within a short time, Jakob introduced me to his family.

Their welcoming smiles were like balls of sunshine, throwing light my way.

Their open arms wrapped around me like rays.

Their conversation and laughter was like a warm, whirling breeze.

Being around Jakob's family felt like being around my own family.

I embraced the joy without question or guilt.

Shortly after that family function, Jakob shared something profound with me, but in a half-joking way. 'You're the kind of person I've always dreamt of marrying,' he said. 'One day, I'm going to win your heart.'

We laughed, and there was a sparkle in my spirit that matched the sparkle in his eye. Although I didn't necessarily love Jakob at that time, I certainly loved being around him. I loved that he brought me to life again. I loved that he melted the cold numbness that had previously frozen me. I loved that he helped me feel joy.

I didn't realise exactly how *much* joy, until I returned to Belgium.

I thought about Jakob all the time. I yearned to see him.

I missed leaning against Jakob, physically and emotionally.

I missed the sunshine in his smile.

And as it turned out, the feelings were mutual.

Jakob and I spoke every day, despite our busy schedules and the time difference. Sometimes we'd only have a quick chat; other times we'd melt into long, easy conversations.

It was during one of these long conversations that Jakob asked me a life-changing question.

'Fiori,' he said. 'Will you marry me?'

In a split second, dozens of thoughts darted through my head.

Fiori, marriage is something you've avoided.

In Eritrea, marriage equalled servitude.

Marriage meant giving up power, choice, and dreams.

Marriage meant pouring all time, effort, and resources into being a wife.

Marriage meant being a young mother.

Marriage meant giving up everything.

But, could it be different with Jakob?

Could it be a loving relationship?

An equal relationship?

You wanted to be a wife and mother ONE day, but on YOUR terms.

When YOU are ready.

That's when I realised something.

I *was* ready.

My heart beat fast. It reminded me that I was alive, truly alive.

'Yes, let's get married, Jakob! Let's do it!'

Within weeks, Jakob came to Belgium. At the airport I held him in my arms.

'We won't be apart for much longer,' he said.

I hoped he was right.

He stayed with me at my apartment, and within days we were married.

The wedding was a small event at the local city hall, followed by an intimate reception at a restaurant. Before our honeymoon, we lodged our official forms for Jakob to sponsor me to live in Australia as his wife. Knowing the forms were in the system helped us enjoy the honeymoon even more. We travelled to Holland, Germany, and France, and to the city of love herself, Paris.

Arriving back to Belgium was bittersweet. We enjoyed returning to my apartment as husband and wife, but before long, Jakob left for Eritrea to visit his sick father. Although I was unable to go (having departed there illegally), Jakob took the opportunity while he was there to introduce himself to my Eritrean family. They liked him straight away, and were thrilled that I was *finally* married!

After Eritrea, Jakob returned to Australia. We spoke every single day, reminiscing about our honeymoon and talking about our impending life together.

We thought it would be a long, twelve-month wait before the application was accepted, but were totally shocked and thrilled when it was approved within two-and-a-half months!

Australia, here I come!

I launched into planning and organisation.

I gave notice at my jobs, sold or got rid of furniture, and generally readied myself for a new life in Australia.

It was so exciting!

Jakob and I still spoke daily. During these calls we'd talk about our day and outline all our to-do tasks.

During one of our daily calls, though, Jakob sounded distracted.

'What's wrong?' I asked.

'Nothing,' he reassured. 'Nothing at all.'

'Tell me,' I said, 'I want to know.'

He sighed. 'Well, I've found a beautiful home for us. I have the deposit of $70,000 (AUD, approximately $50,000 USD) but I need $10,000 more. It looks like we're going to miss out.'

Miss out? No!

I knew Jakob was keen to buy a place for us, but I didn't realise he was already looking. I thought we'd look for a place together, but was thrilled that he'd taken the initiative.

'I have ten thousand in my savings account,' I said. 'I'll send it to you.'

Jakob was quiet for a moment. 'Really, Fiori? Are you sure?'

'Of course I'm sure! This is for our future.'

Jakob showered me with thanks. I could hear the joy in his voice. The words were practically pirouetting out of his mouth.

'I can't wait to move into this home with you, Fiori! To start our new life!'

'I can't wait either.'

Before long, neither of us had to wait. We were both at the Tullamarine airport in Melbourne, hugging.

I was standing in my new country, Australia.

'Come, let's go,' Jakob said, grabbing my bags.

I was looking forward to seeing his apartment for the first time, and staying there until our house came through. My thoughts excitedly sped ahead, imagining how he furnished his apartment. Was his style cool and masculine? Or perhaps traditionally African? He had been so mysterious when I had asked him about it.

When we arrived at his unit block, I could tell it would be neither.

The actual block was old and dirty.

I had heard about Housing Commission blocks from Angesom. He explained they were public units and houses that were partly subsidised by the government for lower income earners. Some of the Housing Commission blocks looked nice, while others looked dingy.

Jakob's block was definitely dingy.

But Jakob wasn't a low income earner? He was a manager. When I asked Jakob if this is where he lived, he nodded vaguely. He also mumbled something about a room.

When I asked for more information, he told me he was illegally sub-letting a small room from two Eritrean brothers.

It wasn't even his unit? He wasn't even on the lease?

Uneasiness coiled in my stomach.

It slithered up to my surprised face.

Jakob saw my shocked expression.

'This is just temporary,' he said.

What was happening?

What was going on?

I swallowed hard.

Thoughts ricocheted around my brain. I asked quietly, nervously: 'When will we be moving into our home?'

Jakob didn't answer straight away. He looked at the floor while picking up some things. 'Not for a while. It's complicated.'

My heart thudded. 'In what way?'

'I'll explain later,' he snapped.

I froze. Jakob had never used a harsh tone with me before. Ever.

I took a deep breath. I continued. 'Please explain it now. We have all the time in the world.'

'Quiet!' he shouted, his teeth glinting. 'The house purchase didn't go as planned. I'm looking for another one!'

I gasped, both from the force of his voice, and the words that fired out.

His eyes were frightening too. It's like all the blood had pumped to his head, making them bloodshot. The whites of his eyes somehow seemed to wave at me like bright, red flags.

A voice in my head said, 'Calm down, it's okay. He's had a big day. He's tired. His life has turned upside down. Don't push it for today.'

So I left it, for that day. But in a couple of days I couldn't wait any longer. The questions were eating away at my brain like termites in a tree trunk. I had waited and waited for a suitable moment when he was in a good mood, but that moment never came. Something was off about Jakob and our entire situation. I had to get to the bottom of it.

'Jakob, how long are we going to live in this room?' I asked. 'What are the plans for buying a house?'

He flung a disdainful look at me. 'We had this conversation the other night. I didn't want to talk about it then, and I don't want to talk about it now.'

'I have a right to know,' I persisted. 'I contributed to the purchase.'

His tone became sharper. His breath quicker. 'I'm working on it.'

I kept my voice calm and gentle, and I continued. I had asked questions all my life; I wasn't going to be suppressed now, by my own husband. 'If the sale fell through, where is the money I sent?'

Jakob's once tender, brown eyes turned into slicks of oil.

He became someone or some*thing* I couldn't recognise.

His eyebrows sliced his forehead like two charcoal blades.

He answered my question, but not with words, with a ferocious slap to the side of my face.

I screamed, first from shock, then from pain.

The slap was so hard it felt like a million needles stabbing my cheek. Large, colourful spots blotted my vision.

I felt like my face would cave in.

My face didn't cave in, but my world certainly did.

CHAPTER SEVEN

SHOCK AND AWE

———⇥●⇤———

Sometimes the most painful walk can

become your most triumphant journey.

A t first, there was shock.

Thunderous shock.

Shock that sent warning messages to every part of my body.

Shock that primed my legs for running, my arms for shielding.

Shock that caused my heart to pound, to palpitate.

Amidst the shock, disbelief flowed fast and freely.

Not just disbelief.

Violation.

Anger.

Sadness.

Guilt.

Shame.

So much shame.

Sludge-like shame that dripped off me, like a glob of saliva.

Memories flashed in my mind too.

Memories of mothers, wives, sisters, daughters—beaten, broken, belittled.

Memories of a bruised Senait hobbling home to our Eritrean village, terrified and alone.

Instantly, I felt united with all of them, in grief and pain.

I'd been initiated into their sad sisterhood. A sisterhood of which I never thought I'd be a part.

I was wrong.

I longed to hold Senait. To be held. To be told that everything would be okay.

'It'll be okay,' he said.

Through my tears, I squinted.

Jakob.

Not the monster with blazing eyes, my loving Jakob.

'Fiori, my darling, I'm so sorry.'

Jakob tried to walk close, but when he saw me recoil, he stopped.

'Please forgive me,' he begged. 'I don't know what happened. I'm so sorry.'

In his eyes I saw the sad, slow dance of regret.

I cried again, this time from relief.

The old Jakob had momentarily left, but now he was back. I cried because I was not like the other women who would be suffering long after Jakob and I made up.

My Jakob wasn't going to hurt me anymore.

He moved forward. This time I didn't flinch.

He held me.

But, something had changed.

His arms felt heavier and tighter, like the bars that restrain you on a roller coaster. Those bars keep you safe if you stay still, but can be painful if you try to wriggle free. Everything's fine as long as you don't escape the spinning, spiralling ride.

'Let me be the man, Fiori. Respect that I'm the man and this won't happen again,' he said. 'You're shaking. I'll get you a cup of tea, something to eat.'

I nodded, relieved that he'd released his arms.

I wasn't hungry or thirsty, but I ate and drank to partake in the peace offering.

I wanted to show I believed, because I did.

Didn't I?

I really *wanted* to believe.

I argued with myself. I reasoned with myself. I warned myself.

For the next few days, my head became the very roller coaster I was strapped to, thoughts whizzing and whirling crazily through my mind—screaming, screeching, shrieking.

After slapping me that day, Jakob had appeared to feel guilty for a few hours, but the guilt then seemed to evaporate.

He became a different man.

Gone was the laid-back Aussie guy whose laugh was like a rainbow. Gone was the gentle man whose soft caresses felt like butterfly wings.

Gone. It was all gone.

In its place, an edginess.

A stress, an impatience, a shortness.

A dominance that demanded an unsettling amount of obedience.

Did I miss something? Had my grief for Amanuel clouded my judgement or smothered my intuition when I first met Jakob?

Had he always been like this?

A bit ... dark?

Had my initial joy at meeting him spread a blinding, beautiful light over his shadows?

Or had he hidden his true self under a mask? A mask he felt comfortable to remove now that I was in Australia? Alone with him? Trapped?

I honestly didn't know.

But I *did* know that more truths were unravelling by the minute.

One day I was curious about Jakob's work attire. Given he was a production manager overseeing twenty-five staff, I wondered why he was wearing a tracksuit. I smiled and said, 'You have a very relaxed office. Isn't there a dress code? I've never worked in an office where the managers wear tracksuits.'

He shrugged. 'These clothes are fine for the factory floor.'

Factory? I didn't care that he worked in a factory, but I cared that he'd lied about it! I felt like he'd thrown a web over me. I couldn't move. I barely knew where I was, and what was happening.

But I *could* see the spider.

Over the coming months, I got to know the insecurities of that spider very well.

And sadly, the ferocity of his bite.

One afternoon I was sitting down in the lounge room chatting to one of the Eritrean brothers who sub-let the room to Jakob.

At one point Jakob came into the room and said to his friend, 'Sorry to interrupt. It's just that I miss my wife and really want some time alone with her.'

His friend thought nothing of it, but there was something threatening in Jakob's tone: a vocal note that trembled like a brandished gun in a holdup.

As soon as we were behind closed doors, Jakob threw me onto the bed.

The action was quick and violent.

He then grabbed my hands and pulled me to my feet, slapping me hard across the face.

I yelped and held my scorching cheek, my eyes wide with shock and fear.

Jakob paced in front of me, glaring.

He then put his face close to mine.

His voice was breathlessly low. He spoke in the same way that fiery smoke slithers threateningly under doorways. 'What are you doing? You are embarrassing me. You are a married woman, my wife. You are making a fool of yourself and *embarrassing* me. This is the first step toward unfaithfulness. Today it's talking; tomorrow it's sex. When are you going to start respecting me?'

It was a rhetorical question because he grabbed me by the throat and pushed me onto the bed.

I fell backward, gasping.

I lay on my back, petrified.

He then left the room in disgust.

I couldn't move.

The ceiling seemed to be spinning.

My thoughts seemed to be spiralling.

What had just happened?

What had I done wrong?

I didn't have much time to think about it, because within minutes, Jakob walked back into the room.

His brow was furrowed. He seemed remorseful, but still annoyed and agitated.

'I love you, Fiori,' he barked, 'and I don't want to hurt you again. But *you* bring this anger out in me. *You* turn me into this person. It won't happen again if you show me respect.'

My brain was starting to slow down.

It took me a moment to absorb his words.

When I did, I instantly felt ashamed that I'd pushed Jakob to do this to me.

Jakob didn't *want* to hurt me.

This was *my* fault. I caused this.

So I changed.

Over the coming weeks I tried hard not to trigger Jakob.

I was careful how I talked to him.

I was careful how I talked to others.

I was careful about everything.

But clearly, I wasn't careful enough.

Even though we eventually moved into our own small apartment, the pattern of abuse continued.

Well, it wasn't a pattern really. A pattern has a gentle ebb and flow. An element of predictability.

Living with Jakob was anything but predictable. His smile could turn into a slither within minutes. His open heart could become an open hand without warning. I felt like a piece of fruit in a blender, never knowing when the switch would flick on.

Even if I stayed low and light, like a butterfly on a leaf, I somehow managed to rattle the tree.

One day Jakob invited one of his friends over for lunch.

I remained a butterfly. I did everything that was expected of me. I cooked a delicious meal and cleaned the apartment thoroughly. When it was time to get dressed, I was careful with my choice of clothes because Jakob was often critical of what I wore. I decided on a blouse and classic-styled pants.

Jakob should approve?

Nope.

'Are you going to the office?' he barked. 'Get changed into something more casual.'

I sighed and went back to my wardrobe.

Looking at the clothes was like staring up a jagged mountain littered with mines. It was dangerous to climb, yet I had to.

I started pulling out some of my casual outfits, deciding to wear a simple skirt and top. I tucked everything in, straightened out the skirt, and then walked out, eyes down.

I waited for the criticism.

It came.

Jakob rolled his eyes. 'Do I introduce you as my wife or my maid?'

I trudged back to the wardrobe.

I removed the skirt and top, feeling drained. With every outfit change, I removed a layer of myself.

This time, I wore leggings and a long-sleeve shirt.

No luck.

'Are you my wife or are you going on a date with him?'

His words ignited my frustration and exhaustion. I couldn't take it anymore. 'What is your problem?' I asked.

My question created an instant, savage reaction in Jakob.

He launched at me, punching me in the stomach.

I felt as though his hand had reached into my chest and squeezed all the air out.

I doubled over and gasped for breath.

I steadied myself on the wall with one hand, and clawed at my stomach with the other.

As I struggled to inhale, I could vaguely hear him screaming and sputtering: 'You are the wife, not the husband! Don't ever talk to me that way again! Show me some respect!'

He then spun around and left.

My mouth was open but no air passed in or out.

For a moment I felt like I was going to die.

But it was just for a moment.

Eventually air, delicious air, started filtering in again.

I crumpled with relief and exhaustion.

I stayed still until I was breathing normally again.

Amidst the sore thudding of my stomach, I decided to get up.

If I wasted too much time, Jakob would get angrier.

The best thing was for me to push the incident out of my mind and focus on being a good wife and a good host.

First, I still had the impossible task of finding something to wear.

I removed a pair of jeans and a t-shirt from a hanger, and slipped them both on.

In the back of my mind I knew it wouldn't be good enough.

It *couldn't* be good enough.

And yet, in the whizzing blender that was my relationship with Jakob, it was.

Maybe he felt calmer after releasing his stress?

He actually smiled.

He even continued to smile when his friend arrived.

The last thing *I* wanted to do was smile. Any joy was winded out of me earlier, but I stretched my lips sweetly for Jakob's friend. I had become good at hiding my real emotions under the scribbled lie that was my smile.

Jakob didn't have to fake his happiness though. He could be whoever he wanted, whenever he wanted, without fear of reprisal.

I envied the way he could release his genuine bliss.

He was so warm and funny. He cracked jokes and shared stories. This was the Jakob I had been attracted to and fallen for.

I wondered how he could so easily slip and slide between two different people.

Jakob even boasted about me to his friend, telling him what a wonderful wife I was.

Joy was flowing from him, thick and fast.

Over the course of the afternoon, some of that joy washed away a part of my misery.

I even felt a shimmer of happiness, especially when hearing him compliment me.

When his friend left, I actually felt so happy that I suggested we go out for a coffee together.

I didn't hear a response.

I put down the dishes and turned around to face Jakob.

Oh no.

He was a bonfire, eyes burning.

My joy went up in smoke.

'What's wrong?' I asked.

'My friend was looking at your arse the whole time.'

My heart scrambled for safety, beating fast. 'What?'

'Every time you walked out of the room, he stared at your butt. You asked for it. You *wanted* it. You didn't wear a long t-shirt to cover your backside. It's your fault.'

'Jakob, please,' I calmed. 'He wasn't looking at me, he really wasn't.'

My words were like water on burning oil.

'Why are you defending him, Fiori?'

Jakob's temper burst into name-calling flames.

Slut.

Whore.

Idiot.

Fool.

I stood there, my eyes filling with tears. Hearing, but trying not to listen.

As much as I hated the pain of being hit, I hated the agony of name-calling even more.

To help fill some of the emptiness in my life, I started doing a retail course at a training college.

The course was interesting, and as always, I enjoyed learning.

But what I wanted most was a part-time job, because I loved interacting with people as well as earning money. Work also fed my self-worth, and given I had so little of it these days, a job was important.

Jakob wasn't keen on the idea at first because he didn't like me making friends and potentially having a good time. But on the other hand, he didn't want me sitting at home being 'lazy' when I wasn't at college, so he eventually welcomed the idea.

With his blessing, I started applying for positions.

It took a while to actually find something, and when I did, it was a fun waitress position in a restaurant. They needed someone to start as soon as possible.

Perfect!

I practically ran out of the house the next morning, ready for my first day.

Working again was absolute bliss. I chatted with the patrons and befriended the staff. I took orders joyfully and carried plates proudly.

That joy stayed with me all the way home, almost twinkling from my skin.

But Jakob had a knack for stripping away my sparkle. 'Don't you know what happens to women who walk home late at night? They get raped. Some of them get murdered.'

The twinkle fizzled.

Over the coming days, Jakob told me more about the terrible things that happened to women after dark. I started questioning whether I should be out so late. Whether I should ask for day shifts instead?

In the end, the decision wasn't up to me.

The bottom line was that Jakob didn't like me working at night, and told me to quit.

I realised, deep down, Jakob ordering me to quit my job was wrong.

I realised, deep down, I had never tolerated such domination and control in the past.

I realised, deep down, I ran away from oppression as a child.

But my realisations were all *so deep down*, that I could barely see or touch the old me under fresh scars and aching bruises.

I couldn't find the lioness. I didn't dare enter her den.

When I quit, I told myself it was *my* decision.

I told myself it was dangerous for me to walk home late at night.

I told myself that safety was my priority.

I lied to myself to relieve some of the shame.

It didn't work. The lies just fuelled my embarrassment.

The only way to salvage some of my dignity was to get another job.

I scoured the papers and online sites, and eventually got a job working as an administrative assistant for a doctor.

The job was during daylight hours, so Jakob approved.

The doctor worked in private practice as well as a hospital, so my position included scheduling, making appointments, and completing day-to-day business tasks.

Despite the person I was around Jakob, I hatched out of my shell at work.

I *loved* the job, but this time I kept all the excitement to myself. I didn't want Jakob to fill my head with scary stories or order me to quit. Before I walked through the front door each night, I'd exhale all my joy like a car tyre losing air. I didn't have to pretend to be flat. Walking through the door was like getting caught in a net of sadness that trapped me until it was time to break free the next morning.

And thankfully, every morning, I did break free.

Everything was going reasonably well until one evening my boss sent me a text.

Jakob snatched the phone and read the message out loud: 'Thank you for organising the files I needed. I'm really happy with your work.'

I opened my mouth to speak, but he jumped in.

I could already feel the job slipping from my fingers.

'Why is your boss sending you texts at night? Why is he so happy? What are you *doing* to make him happy? What's going on between you two?'

'Nothing! Read the text again,' I begged. 'It is completely innocent. He has an important meeting tomorrow and I got something ready for him, that's all.'

'Two weeks into your job,' he snarled, 'and you're getting personal messages from your boss who is SO happy with you. You need to quit right now.'

My heart sank.

I sank.

Even my voice seemed to fall deep into my throat.

I felt as though I was falling from a tall building in slow motion. As I fell, I saw people in offices continuing to work, while I plummeted further and further away from them, into darkness.

I noted the irony.

I had defied my destiny of marrying a man in Africa because I didn't want to be controlled like a puppet. I fled Eritrea because I didn't want to die in a war or erode in my destiny. I left city after city to protect my safety.

And yet, here I was, under the heavy thumb of a violent, overbearing, unreasonable man.

Every moment of every day, I felt more fear, more shame, more self-loathing.

When I looked in the mirror, I no longer saw the girl who once defied her destiny. I saw a married woman, melting away into misery.

I no longer saw the lioness who had fled her country to escape violence and murder. I saw a scared kitten in a suburban war zone.

I no longer saw the female who'd taken a plane from Belgium to shake herself free from grief. I saw a prisoner of domestic violence, trapped behind the bars of a loveless marriage.

I didn't like what I saw.

But shame and fear stopped me from doing anything about it.

———————⟶●⟵———————

I quite liked Jakob's mum.

Even though I couldn't tell her about the abuse I was experiencing, I had very few friends in Australia, and I enjoyed her company.

One particular day when I visited her, she told me about a cockroach problem she was having.

'Don't worry Mum,' I said, 'we also have a few cockroaches in our apartment. We'll research a way to get rid of them for you.'

That night I spoke to Jakob about the cockroaches.

'You told my Mum we had cockroaches?' he snapped.

I was about to speak but thought better of it.

For some reason, he was turning into a volcano.

'Why would you tell my mother we have cockroaches?!' he yelled. 'She's going to think you're a lazy wife. Why do you embarrass me like this over and over again? When will you learn? When will you respect me?'

He erupted, unleashing his lava.

His mouth spewed out a hot river of insults.

You are dirty.

You are unorganised.

You are lazy.

You are stupid.

You are brainless.

You are DUMB.

You are shameless.

You are disrespectful.

You are an IDIOT.

The lava devoured me.

It singed my self-worth.

It disintegrated my dignity.

I needed to leave the house quickly or I'd drown in his burning hatred. 'I'm going for a drive,' I said, my voice wobbling.

'Fucking bitch, you're not going anywhere.'

I froze. He wasn't going to let me leave.

What now?

I was stuck.

I would have to do *something*.

I know—I'll try reasoning with him. 'Baby, you're blowing my conversation with your mum out of proportion. You're exaggerating for no good reason.'

It was time for another eruption, bigger and more destructive than the last.

In an instant, he pushed me hard onto the dining table.

I then fell from the table onto a stool, finally onto the floor.

My head and hip smarted from the pain.

Jakob then walked up to me and pressed his foot onto my face.

I screamed at him to please stop.

The smell of his shoe was now all over my skin.

I *became* the smell.

I became the chewing gum that annoyingly sticks to the bottom of people's shoes.

He then put his foot on my throat.

How did I end up here? On the floor? Figuratively under my husband's thumb, and *literally* under his foot?

I thought of the incident in Libya, when someone spat on my ankle.

I felt such shame.

Their spit was filthy.

Now, I *was* the spit. I *was* the filth.

'Never tell me I'm exaggerating again,' Jakob warned. 'You bring me so much grief. You embarrass me constantly. Never tell me I'm exaggerating again. Do you understand?'

I tried my best to nod.

He removed his foot.

I could breathe properly again, but I felt dirty.

Worthless.

And my worth continued to plummet.

The next time Jakob abused me, he filled a glass of water and threw it in my face. The fast, wet splash felt like a slap. A slap that was far more humiliating than one delivered by hand. I stood there, water dripping from my nose and hair. Self-worth dripping from my soul.

On another occasion, Jakob pulled my hair and ordered me to call a male friend from Sudan to tell him never to contact me again. Jakob was pulling my hair *while* I was talking to my friend. I felt as though my scalp would tear away.

These are just a couple of examples.

The abuse was getting so bad, I contemplated leaving.

But how could I, when *I* was the problem?

How could I leave when I should feel grateful he stayed with me, despite all my faults?

How could I, when surely only weak women end up in these violent situations in the first place?

How could I, when I was petrified of what he'd do to me if I left?

After a particular incident though, as scared as I was, I knew I needed help.

Jakob was angry with me, as usual. On this particular night, though, he began to drink.

I hated it when he drank.

He began unleashing threats.

I'm going to destroy your face.

I'm going to break your neck.

I'm going to make sure no one recognises you.

I'm going to make sure your life is a misery.

'I'm scared,' I said, trembling, walking to the door. 'I need to leave for a little while.'

Jakob leapt to the door before I could get there.

He locked the internal dead bolt, pulled the keys out, and kept them. 'You're not going anywhere. If you try to leave, I'll kill you.'

I was locked in.

I was his prisoner.

I was terrified.

No matter how much I pleaded to be let out, he refused.

That's when I said something I've never said before: 'Please open the door or I'll call the police.'

He laughed. 'You? Call the police? Sure, go ahead and do that.'

So I did. I went to the bedroom, pulled out my phone with shaking hands, and made the call in a low voice.

He didn't think for a minute I'd call, and by the time he casually walked in, I'd finished.

'The police are on their way,' I warned, my heart hammering.

He looked at me with huge eyes.

He swore at me.

Shouted.

But, surprisingly, he wasn't overly concerned that the authorities were coming.

'The police won't do anything,' he spat. 'You don't have any bruises. I'll talk my way out of it. When they're gone, you'll pay.'

The blood drained from my body.

Jakob was probably right.

The fact that I didn't have bruises and breaks was one of the reasons I justified staying with Jakob. I told myself that things could be worse, that a slap here and a punch there were nothing. Other women had to contend with so much more.

I immediately regretted making the call.

If the police left without doing anything, what would happen to me?

I would soon find out, because there was a knock.

Jakob opened the door and after letting the male and female officer in, he immediately turned on the charm. 'I love my wife,' he gushed. 'I would never hurt her.'

The female officer asked me if I was okay.

I didn't know how to answer that question.

When I first called, I was planning to tell them everything. I wanted to detail the abuse I'd endured over our five months together. But now, how could I? Where was my proof? I had no bruises, no breaks. Jakob had scared me into silence.

Yet, I had to say something.

I simply replied, 'He threatened me. He was drinking. He locked me in the house and wouldn't let me leave.'

The female officer questioned Jakob about this.

'Sure, we had a fight,' he said, shrugging. 'All couples do. And yes, I was drinking at home but that's not a crime. I only locked the door because I didn't want her to drive while being upset, because she might have an accident. But I won't do that again.'

Jakob then handed me the keychain which had my car and front door keys on them.

I swear, Jakob could have won an Oscar!

The male officer believed every word Jakob said. He turned to me, 'Your husband was only trying to protect you by keeping you indoors. As for the drinking, he's in his house so he's not breaking any laws. You can leave now, you have the keys, and you can call us at any time if the situation changes.'

The police then left, and I felt like they'd taken a piece of my soul with them.

But I didn't stay.

I followed them out. I wasn't hanging around Jakob. Instead, I drove to his mother's house. I couldn't tell her what had happened because she would side with her son, so I just told her I was out for a drive.

I would have loved to have driven to a close friend or family member's house, but didn't have anyone like that in Melbourne.

Unfortunately, I couldn't stay with Jakob's mum forever, so I eventually left.

I hoped by the time I got home that Jakob would be asleep or passed out.

No.

Neither.

As soon as I walked through the door, his face was a canvas of lightning and thunder.

I was in the eye of his storm.

He grabbed my throat.

I started gasping for breath.

I instantly wished I had told the police everything.

I wished I'd stayed away.

I wished I'd gone anywhere but home.

Jakob had an expression I'd never seen before.

Dark. Calculated.

It was then that he showed me a knife.

He held it close. I could see its serrated blade.

I could almost smell the steel.

I started whimpering and crying.

'If you ever call the police again, I will kill you,' he whispered. 'I will actually kill you. The cops will never believe your stories. I will always talk my way out of it, and when they're gone, you'll be dead.'

The words slithered out of his throat and coiled around my neck.

My body started to shake.

Fear was thrashing in my stomach.

I wanted to be sick.

I stared at Jakob's dilated pupils for minutes, silent, but screaming on the inside.

Just as I wondered whether I would survive the night, he broke his gaze and reunited with his beer bottle.

I exhaled and held my stomach, willing myself not to vomit.

Jakob didn't hit me.

That should be good news, but it wasn't.

It was bad, very bad.

Often after he hit me, there was a sense of calm. A sense of quiet for a day or two, or even weeks. A sense of balance, because he got his anger out, and I got what I deserved. (Until I did something wrong again, which tilted the scales, forcing him to bring everything back into alignment.)

But there was no balance tonight.

There was instability. An ominous unease.

Cold.

Brewing.

Silent.

I almost *wished* he'd hit me, because the unknown was more frightening.

It was excruciating.

Tormenting.

I wanted it to end.

Two days later, it did.

Jakob wanted money. To be exact, he wanted $18,500, which he claimed was to pay a debt.

He had asked for money several times before, and I had given it, but never this amount. I always suspected he had gambling debts but was too afraid to ask.

'We are married, Fiori. Your money is my money, right?'

I didn't know what to say.

Thoughts were scrambling around my head.

What do I do?

Thank God it's Sunday and the banks are closed.

My silence was a bad idea.

He launched at me.

He pushed me against the wall and held my throat.

Like last time, he pulled a knife out from behind his back, but this time he pushed it against my skin.

I wanted to scream, but could barely breathe.

This was it. Today I would die.

I felt the cold blade against my neck. It was like a scalpel, ready to slice me in two.

My eyes were bulging out of their sockets from fear and horror.

My heartbeat was like an out-of-control locomotive.

'Don't tell *anyone* I've asked you for money. Don't bother calling the police—they'll do nothing, you know it, and then you'll be dead. Do you understand?'

I nodded, trying to move as little as possible.

Waves of hot fear bubbled on my forehead.

Jakob's canon-ball pupils bore into my soul.

My brows dripped with sweat.

Then, when he could see nothing but terror in my face, he pulled away.

He may have released his grip, but his eyes still held my gaze.

He glared at me as he picked up his bag. He then walked out the door.

As his hate lingered in the air, I fell to the floor.

I allowed myself to gasp for breath.

I lay in the foetal position, shaking, throbbing, crying.

The banging between my ears was so loud, I had to hold my head, clench my scalp.

Tears were soaking my cheeks.

When I was all cried out, I slowly sat up and used my singlet to wipe my face. I wasn't sure how I'd have the energy to ever stand again. I stared zombie-like at my legs; that's when I caught a glimpse of something on my knee.

It was probably invisible to anyone else, but to me, it was like a blazing, neon sign.

It was the speck of a scar.

A scar born from school beatings and military punishment.

A scar born from challenging the system, standing up for what was right, and defying my destiny.

It was a scar that reminded me I *always* got back up, no matter how often I was pushed down.

A scar that I'd decided, all those years ago, would be my map of resilience.

I had misplaced that map since moving to Australia. It had become buried under layers of doubt.

But now, as I wandered, lost and alone in the wilderness of defeat, it appeared before me.

The scar was small, but it was like an arrow, and it pointed straight to the door.

I realised in that instant, past pain was my pathway.

Every bump and bruise was a coordinate.

Pain showed me a way out *if* I chose to follow the map.

The door to my freedom was closing more and more every day.

I had to leave.

It was now or never.

A moment ago, I thought I would live the rest of my life on the bathroom floor, too weak to rise.

Now, I would fight, as I always had.

I dragged myself to my feet despite my head erupting.

I steadied myself against the sink.

I walked to the bedroom, put some clothes on, and packed a small bag.

Although I felt nauseous and dizzy, I kept standing, I kept moving.
I followed my map through the door.
I put one foot in front of the other.
I left Jakob.

Without the love and support of close friends or family in
Melbourne, I went straight to the police station, alone.

Once there, I asked to speak with a female officer. I hoped
she'd understand the predicament I was in, rather than siding with
Jakob as the male officer had done at our apartment.

I was told I could speak to a female officer, but that I'd have to
wait until one became available, which could be a while.

I looked over my shoulder. 'Can you please hide me in your
office until then, or put me at the back of the station? He might
come here; he might kill me.'

The officer reassured me. 'No one is going to kill you in the
police station, but if you're concerned, you can come and wait
inside one of the rooms.'

The knots in my shoulder released, but moths battled in my
stomach as I waited in the room.

After an hour, a female officer finally came. She was friendly
and comforting, and listened carefully to my complaint. With
her help, I set the wheels in motion to get an intervention order
against Jakob, which is a legal order stopping him from coming

near me. I was also given information about the nearest women's refuge. The officer made a call to them and within a short time, a person came and picked me up.

As I sat in the car on the way to the refuge, I called my parents from my mobile.

I didn't want to. They had no idea I'd been physically and emotionally abused. Now, despite the shame, I had to tell them. My safety depended on it.

I tried to condense the last five months into five minutes.

Naturally, my mum and dad were in total shock.

I couldn't comfort them.

My main message was: don't contact Jakob or answer any of his calls.

They understood and made me promise to stay in touch whenever it was safe to do so.

I promised, but at that moment, I had no idea when I'd be safe again.

When we arrived at the refuge, I almost missed seeing it. It was like an everyday suburban family home. However, behind the picket fence was a wall of secrets.

I became one of those secrets, hiding away in order to stay alive.

As I walked through the door, everyone was friendly. They greeted me with a smile.

A *knowing* smile. A smile that said, 'We understand your sense of worthlessness. We know your pain. We feel your fear.'

I could see the shame on some of their faces too.

Their shame was an open book. I could read the words.

I did something wrong to be here.

I feel weak and pathetic.

I feel helpless.

I should have left sooner.

I am nothing.

I am no one.

Shame, shame ... so much shame.

And yet, now that I was out of the house and away from Jakob, I instantly saw things differently.

I no longer felt shame.

We—the ladies and I—should *not* feel shame.

We should feel courage and pride.

We didn't cause the problems.

We didn't ask to be slapped.

We didn't ask to be taunted.

We didn't ask to be emotionally abused.

We were the victims, not the perpetrators.

We were brave to stay.

We were brave to run.

Either way, we did what was necessary to stay alive.

I smiled back at the ladies, and for the first time in months, with pride.

Shortly after arriving, I was taken aside and given some preliminary information from the on-duty social worker.

There were a lot of details about chores and rules. One of the most important rules was to *never* disclose the address of the refuge. To do so would endanger everyone's lives. The refuge wasn't there to keep vulnerable women in; it was there to keep angry partners *out*.

I understood that perfectly.

I was shown my room, which was furnished with two beds, a small table and a mirror.

I was emotionally and physically exhausted, so I flopped on the bed. Given how tired I was, I assumed that sleep would cradle me immediately.

It didn't.

Something else held me in its heavy, cold arms.

Jakob.

Or rather, thoughts of Jakob.

Visions of the knife slashed my thoughts.

I jumped up.

I put my head in my hands and rubbed my banging temples, trying to erase images of the glinting blade.

But I couldn't; I just couldn't.

I walked around. The only answer was to keep myself busy and keep my mind occupied.

I had to take action and focus on the solutions rather than the problem.

It was hard, but I had to try.

I got on the internet, made calls, completed tasks.

I changed my phone number and texted the new number to my parents and a few close friends in Belgium.

I called different legal firms, and selected a lawyer to meet with.

I started looking online for a secondhand car and earmarked one to inspect.

Being busy helped.

When night eventually came, mercifully, I fell asleep.

But after a few hours I woke up, gasping and clutching my throat. Adrenaline flooded through my body causing my fingers and toes to tingle and sizzle.

I'd had a nightmare. In it, Jakob had hacked away at me. He pulled out my voice box so I could no longer speak.

My voice—the one tool I used my whole life to question, to argue, to fight—was ripped out of me.

I sat up and shook for an hour.

I eventually tried to go back to sleep.

I tossed and turned.

I counted, sang, hummed.

Jakob still controlled me. He was everywhere. Haunting me. Harassing me.

When morning came, I welcomed the rays with baggy eyes and a foggy mind.

I walked around in a daze.

Every time a flashback struck, I'd sweat, breathe fast, feel dizzy.

I'd start panicking about the current situation.

What was Jakob doing right now?

Was he scouring the streets looking for me?

Was he calling everyone to track me down?

I could only imagine his rage.

I texted my mum to ask if he'd contacted her.

Yes, he had.

He'd called all my family, and even friends in Belgium. He'd outlined in great and grotesque detail how he was going to kill me if I didn't stop the intervention order. Some of my friends even encouraged me to abandon the proceedings because they were frightened for my safety.

My hands trembled as I read their messages.

My breathing became shallow and fast.

How would I ever get out of this situation alive?

Over the next few weeks, I asked myself that question constantly.

My nights were filled with nightmares.

My days were filled with nightmares as well, ones that I could not escape from.

And just when I thought things couldn't get any worse, they did.

One night I experienced the worst pain I'd ever experienced in my life.

My stomach felt like it was being ripped apart by steel claws.

I collapsed and clutched myself.

I wretched.

On this particular night the social worker was located elsewhere but contactable by phone, so I yelped at one of the nearby women to please call an ambulance.

Instead, she rang the social worker to ask if it was okay to contact emergency services, given the strict privacy policy.

I could hear the woman's end of the conversation from where I was lying: 'So if Fiori pays for the ambulance herself, it's fine? I can call?'

She hung up the phone and ran back into the room.

I didn't wait for her to speak.

'Yes! I'll pay! Just please get me an ambulance!'

She did, but I had to writhe around on the floor for nearly forty-five minutes till the ambulance arrived. The whole time I thought my insides would get sucked into the scraping, clawing, crushing pain.

When the paramedics finally came, I was given something for the pain, then passed out. I woke up in a hospital room where a doctor was filling in some paperwork.

She spoke to me and started asking questions. She took my blood pressure and temperature, completed some tests, then left.

I lay there, groggy, but still exploding on the inside.

When the doctor returned later, she told me there were no physical reasons for the pain. Oh, and also, asked me to leave straight away!

I nearly burst into tears. 'Straight away? Please! I'm still in agony.'

'I'm sorry but we've done as many tests as we can. We need this bed for other patients. You're taking up a bed.'

What?!

I wanted to confirm I'd heard correctly, but she had gone.

I stared at the empty doorway for minutes as my insides thrashed.

Breathless with pain and speechless with worry, I eventually came to a realisation.

The doctor had found nothing wrong with me because there *was* nothing wrong with me.

Not with my physical body, anyway.

The psychological trauma had created physical trauma. I'd seen this in a few soldiers at the military hospital.

My emotional pain had manifested into physical agony.

I had quite literally become 'worried sick.'

And I was *still* worried sick.

I felt totally alone.

Unloved.

Unimportant.

I had no one.

No one to hold my hand and tell me everything would be okay.

No one to get me a mediocre cup of coffee or an over-priced hospital sandwich.

No one to pick me up and take me somewhere safe.

I couldn't even catch a bus back to the refuge because I had no money or wallet.

The pain was still ripping at my stomach.

But in the depths of the discomfort, I thought about something.

I remembered a time, years ago, when I stood at the cold, watery lip of Libya's ocean.

The freezing wind drilled into my bones that night, but I felt slightly warmer when I stopped focusing on the cold, and started looking ahead to a brighter, warmer future.

Today, my perception had to shift again.

As hard as it was, it just *had* to.

I refocused.

I accepted the situation for what it was.

I couldn't change the past. I couldn't predict the future. I could only survive in the moment.

I realised that I had to help myself, because no one in this hospital was going to do a damn thing for me.

I sat up, which seemed to require the strength of lifting a car. I clutched myself, almost losing consciousness from the pain.

I got off the bed, and stood.

I steadied myself.

I'd brought nothing with me to the hospital, but I left with something—refocus, resolve, resilience.

I drew on those qualities as I somehow walked *ten* long, aching kilometres back to the refuge.

With every step I took, I felt as though I was being punched in the guts with steel-knuckled gloves.

I kept walking though.

I put one foot in front of the other, as I've always done.

After five excruciating hours, I dragged myself through the doors of the refuge.

It was the most painful walk of my life, and yet one of my most triumphant journeys ever.

Earlier, I'd told myself if I hobbled through those doors alive, I could achieve anything.

I believed that with all my heart.

My thoughts had been reframed.

My life *would* be transformed.

———————>>●<——————

The next day, I was still in pain, but much less.

I wasn't going to spend my day lying in bed when there was so much to do.

I tucked my hair under a big hat to disguise myself and armed myself with pepper spray.

I was terrified, but I went out anyway.

Jakob seemed to be everywhere: in my head, over my shoulder, and around every corner. He was like a shadow, staining the paths and painting the walls. Creeping and crouching, ready to pounce.

My greatest fear was that he'd see me, grab me, and drag me back to the apartment where he'd kill me.

I could never return to his clutches.

I could never walk into that dungeon again.

I walked into a car dealership instead.

I purchased the secondhand car I'd seen online.

I then drove to a law firm and hired a lawyer.

I walked into a real estate agent's office and looked for a place to rent.

There, the momentum slowed.

I hit a brick wall.

The conversation started positively, but when the agent found out I didn't have a full-time job or a history of paying rent in Australia, he said he couldn't help.

'What if I show you my job history in Belgium?' I asked, pulling out my paperwork.

He glanced at it briefly and shook his head. 'We don't accept papers from other countries. Besides it's all in Dutch.'

'What about my bank savings?'

The agent narrowed his eyes suspiciously. 'How do I know it's not drug money?'

I crinkled my forehead.

Seriously?

I was astounded he'd think such a thing, let alone say it to my face?

Once again I was the black girl with dark intentions.

'I worked my fingers to the bone to earn that money,' I stated. 'I lived on very little each week, and saved carefully. That's not drug money.'

He shrugged. 'I still can't help you.'

During the course of the day, various real estate agents told me pretty much the same thing.

No one could help me.

I was deflated, but not defeated.

I couldn't dwell on the problem.

I had to focus on the solution.

The next morning I posted an ad on a home share site. Within hours, a lady named Renata contacted me about a room in her South Yarra apartment.

I was overjoyed, but I was also upfront. 'Renata, I need to be honest. I only want the room for three months. During that time I'm going to get a job and find my own place. At the end of the three months I'd like a letter from you stating that I've made regular and punctual payments. Is that okay with you?' (Little did I realise we'd happily live with each other for nearly eighteen months!)

'Of course, totally fine,' Renata said. 'When can you move in?'

'Straight away!'

All the pieces were falling into place.

Within a week I'd secured the room with Renata, found a job as a food and beverage attendant at Crown Casino, and also started martial arts classes.

It's amazing how quickly my confidence started growing, when only weeks earlier I lay crumpled on the bathroom floor.

I learnt to walk tall again.

I felt unstoppable and invincible.

But there was one *big* problem.

Soon, I would have to face Jakob in court.

CHAPTER EIGHT

POWER AND PASSION

Fear thrives when dreaded,

and dies when confronted.

When I saw Jakob for the first time in court, his eyes were like two claws scraping down the bare bone of my spine.

He was a rolling ball of thunder.

A stirring sea of hate.

A horizon drenched in shadows.

He'd risen from the depths of my nightmares to walk inside the courtroom.

He was now sitting just metres away.

As I glanced at him, fragments of sharp, painful memories splintered my mind like a cracked mirror.

My heart became a tornado. I shook from its ferocity.

But as sweat drenched my palms, I realised something.

I left Jakob.

The power was in *my* hands.

If he had a hold on me, it's because I was letting him.

I couldn't let him.

I *wouldn't* let him.

He'd beaten me. He'd weakened me. He'd suppressed me.

But I broke free.

And when I came to this realisation, just like that, the mighty wings of my inner eagle quelled the tornado. My rapid breaths eased into controlled inhalations. My rattling body relaxed and stilled. The broken pieces of the mirror became whole, and in it, I saw my reflection.

I saw Fiori Giovanni.

A woman who was scared, yet strong. Nervous, yet determined.

And that scared, strong, nervous, determined woman was ready for the fight of her life.

I *had* to fight because Jakob was contesting the intervention order, and I could see he planned to battle with the might of an army. His side of the courtroom was filled with friends, family, and acquaintances. My side contained just me, my lawyer, and a volunteer from the refuge.

The courtroom was lopsided for many of those early appearances. Sometimes I'd look around at the empty chairs behind me and visualise my family and friends sitting there, as well as my grandmothers and great-grandmothers past.

I missed them, and wished they were with me, but I didn't *need* their presence to win the case.

I just needed courage. And a committed, professional lawyer.

I had the courage, but unfortunately, I didn't have the appropriate lawyer.

I had initially chosen my lawyer from a dazzling portfolio of images at the law firm. Choosing her was tough, because I had to make my selection based on nothing but photos and an hourly rate. I asked one of the partners in the firm which associate was the best. She simply replied, 'They're all excellent.'

Great, narrows it down perfectly!

I eventually made my choice based on the fact that my lawyer seemed a bit nerdy! I assumed this would translate to professionalism and drive.

I was dead wrong.

To my disbelief, outside the courtroom, Jakob got one of his friends to start complimenting my lawyer on her looks.

My lawyer instantly fell for the man's charms.

One day as we were preparing for court, she was completely distracted. Her head was floating around in heart-shaped clouds as she was telling me how handsome Jakob's friend was, and how he kept showering her with compliments.

She then told me she was looking forward to their date.

Their *date?*

She was *going out* with him?

I thought this was extremely unprofessional, and fired her, fast.

I returned to the law firm, this time hiring a lawyer named Phillip. After our first meeting, I could tell he was laser-focused on getting justice for me, and wouldn't be distracted by any of Jakob's tricks.

But it wasn't going to be easy, as we found out in court.

Jakob paid 'witnesses' to get up on the stand and tell the judge what a wonderful, caring, gentle person he was. Some of his witnesses even told the judge *I* had been abusive to *him.*

When I heard the lies, I clenched my fists.

My lawyer sensed my anger. He just smiled and said, 'Relax. When you tell the truth, you don't have to remember your lies. Watch them forget.'

I watched. I listened. I learned. I smiled.

Under cross examination, Phillip asked very specific questions to the first witness, nailing him down on details, times, and events.

Phillip then requested a break.

When we came back from the break, Phillip asked the witness to return to the stand, and proceeded to ask *exactly* the same questions. By this time though, the witness had completely forgotten his story. Phillip seized on this, pouncing on the man's conflicting details and contradictory statements.

The witness stuttered and stammered, backtracked and side stepped.

Phillip followed a similar formula for every one of Jakob's people, including Jakob himself.

Eventually they all tripped over their lies and floundered in their falsehoods.

As time went on, Jakob asked less and less people to be at the courtroom.

He was losing.

He knew it.

His case was being dismantled by Phillip, which in the process was reinforcing *my* case, as well as my self-esteem.

Added to this, I was continuing with martial arts.

I was getting stronger, physically and mentally—which was just as well, because the court case dragged on for ten exhausting months.

Regardless, we brought our A-game to every single appearance.

Phillip looked strong.

I looked strong.

The case looked strong.

And just when the judge was ready to make her ruling, Jakob's lawyer quickly asked the judge if she could speak briefly to her client.

The lawyer was given permission, and immediately started whispering to Jakob.

It turns out, she was advising Jakob to voluntarily consent to the intervention order, knowing the case was weak, and that he'd be found guilty. She proposed instead that he consent to the intervention order without admission of guilt.

The judge was happy with that.

I was happy with that.

Phillip was happy with that.

Our main goal was to get the intervention order, and we got it.

Although Jakob could have voluntarily consented to the order ten months before without the need for a drawn-out court case, I had to focus on the fact that he eventually granted it. I had to focus on the positives.

The main positive was: I won.

I defeated Jakob.

He used several dirty tricks, but justice prevailed.

The *truth* prevailed.

But, there was another court case yet to win. This court case was a criminal case between the police and Jakob.

When I first went to the police, prior to moving to the women's refuge, I told them I didn't want to press charges against Jakob. I didn't want to drag him into the criminal justice system and potentially ruin his life; I just wanted him to leave me alone. I just did not want to see him again, ever.

Not pressing charges turned out to be a bad move, because in the early days of the intervention order court case, he would often say, 'If I'm guilty, why isn't she asking the police to charge me?'

It was disappointing that Jakob used my well-intentioned decision against me. It was reckless too, because I returned to the police station and asked them to indeed charge Jakob.

The police weren't keen on doing that, because their preference had been to charge him earlier. But as I'd made a formal request, they had to follow through.

They contacted Jakob and asked him to come in to the police station for a quick chat.

The problem for Jakob was, some time had passed since the event and he had forgotten the fabricated story he'd first told them. As a result, the short chat turned into a much longer conversation, and at the end, the police were keen to lay charges.

By the time the criminal case came around, which was two months after the intervention order case, Jakob had lost his confidence. Instead of claiming to be innocent, he pled guilty and made a deal even before I was called as a witness.

I can't remember the exact punishment he received, but it was possibly a fine as well as some community service. The punishment was irrelevant though, because justice had been served.

From the moment I walked out on Jakob, he wanted to fight me, hurt me, and defeat me. But his vindictiveness actually made me stronger.

Made me a winner.

I savoured the wins, giving credit to my lawyer, and also to myself. I had faced up to the man who threatened to kill me. But I had walked away tougher and more resilient than ever before.

Now, it was time to sever all ties with Jakob.

More than anything, I wanted to lose the title of 'wife.'

Just days after Jakob had granted the order, I began filling out the divorce papers.

With every sentence I wrote, I felt relieved.

With every box I ticked, I felt empowered.

I was whizzing through the form, but one question made me stop.

Made me think.

It was a question about property division. Although we had no property to divide, I *had* given Jakob $10,000 (AUD) for a supposed house deposit. But we never got a house, and I never saw that money again.

He'd actually asked for money of varying amounts on several occasions, but I had no proof of those payments. For the house deposit though, I had my bank statement.

As much as I wanted to cut ties with Jakob, I didn't want him having a piece of something that was rightfully mine, so I put the $10,000 in the property division section of the form, and waited for his response.

Of course, he refused. He probably had spent the money ages ago, even before I arrived in Australia.

Well, now I wanted it back, and if that meant going to court again, so be it. I could handle it.

In fact, since I'd already invested thousands of dollars hiring a lawyer for the previous court case, I decided to represent *myself* in court for this one.

It was a big step.

A daunting step.

But a step I could handle.

In an interesting twist, Jakob also decided to represent himself.

It was literally Fiori versus Jakob, head to head.

The courtroom would be our boxing ring.

The gloves would be off.

It would be a symbolic showdown.

On the date of our court case, I walked in to see Jakob sitting smugly in his chair on his side of the courtroom.

I'm sure he thought I'd be a trembling, bumbling mess without the support of a lawyer.

I'm sure he thought he could intimidate and scare me.

I'm sure he thought he could knock me down with one malicious, attacking line after another.

I'm sure he thought I'd cower when I put him on the stand.

I'm sure he thought many things, none of which eventuated.

I *did* put him on the stand though, and once there, he sat up straight and tall with an air of cockiness and superiority.

At the edge of his mouth, a small smirk curled like a fish hook, ready to snare.

I wouldn't take the bait.

Finally, this was a fair fight. I stood squarely in front of him, my shoulders back, my eyes piercing into his.

'Jakob, I have a bank statement that shows I deposited $10,000 from my Belgium bank account into your bank account. Where is the money? I want it back.'

His smirk fell away.

The firmness in my voice rattled him. Where was the shaking, shivering mess he was expecting? She certainly wasn't standing in front of him in this courtroom. In fact, I felt like a cobra, my words ready to flare and strike at any moment.

Jakob recovered from his surprise.

He cleared his throat and prepared for his show.

'That money wasn't yours,' he stated. 'I brought that money from Australia to Belgium.'

'Where is the proof showing that you withdrew $10,000 from an account?'

'I don't have any proof.'

'Why not?'

The once-smooth caramel in his voice started heating up, bubbling at the edges. 'It was money I saved. I stored it at home ... in cash.'

'Where did you store it?'

'Under my mattress,' he said, trying to work out how to regain control.

'Why didn't you deposit it in a bank?'

He began fidgeting. 'I like to have cash at home, in case I need to lend money to my family or friends.'

'You can withdraw money from a bank though, right?'

'I didn't want to.'

'Fine, so you claim you had the money when coming to see me in Belgium. When you were on the plane, you would have had to fill out a form declaring that you have $10,000 or more in cash. Did you declare the $10,000 you supposedly had?'

He shifted in his seat. 'No.'

'Why not?'

He seemed hesitant now. 'I guess I didn't see that question.'

Up until this point I had remained calm. But man, I was so sick of his bullshit! My cobra head flared, and I struck. 'It's right there on the page! Even a five-year-old can read it! So answer me this, are you an idiot? Or are you a liar?'

He opened his mouth, but no words came out.

'Answer me!' I ordered. 'Are you such an idiot that you couldn't read a line staring you right in the face? Or are you just a liar, because it wasn't your money in the first place? Idiot or liar? Which one are you?'

Jakob looked like a dazed fighter after a near-knockout punch. He looked up helplessly at the judge. 'Your Honour, she asked for an intervention order, saying that she was afraid of me, but if she's so afraid, how could she be speaking to me like this?'

Hot venom rushed through my veins. 'I'm not afraid of you anymore, you scumbag!'

Again, Jakob whipped his head up to look at the judge. 'Your Honour! She is yelling at me! She is insulting me!'

Jakob wanted her to call off the fight.

She didn't.

Instead, she turned to me and asked, ''Scumbag' has different meanings. Which one are you referring to in reference to the defendant?'

I was a bit surprised by her question, and the calmness of its delivery.

'Sorry, I don't know what the different meanings are? I just know that he's a scumbag.'

'A scumbag can mean that he's an unpleasant person who has done something dishonest,' she explained, 'or that he acts like a lowlife who treats people badly.'

Jakob's jaw dropped as he listened to our conversation.

'Both,' I answered. 'He's both.'

She nodded. 'Return to your questioning.'

The judge didn't intervene. She didn't demand I change my language. She didn't order me to control my tone. She obviously felt my approach was warranted.

So I continued.

I asked question after question. Jakob answered them, but in a rattled, angry way that didn't look good for him, or his case.

With every dishonest answer, he knitted himself into an impenetrable thicket of lies.

He was flustered.

He floundered.

And when the judge eventually made her ruling in my favour, he was outraged.

I, on the other hand, was ecstatic!

I wanted to cry tears of joy. I didn't though—I had cried too many tears in front of Jakob. Now, it was time for a triumphant smile.

There was hardly anyone in the courtroom, but I felt as though every person I loved was there in spirit—even Amanuel, or *especially* Amanuel—standing up and cheering for me, clapping and waving. Together, we celebrated a courageous fight and a fair win.

This win was especially triumphant because *I* won this on my own.

But we weren't done yet.

After the ruling, the judge spoke directly to Jakob. She asked him questions relating to money.

I realised, during the course of her questioning, the sort of measures Jakob had taken to avoid paying me if he lost the case.

It turns out, as soon as he'd received the summons, he opted for a redundancy (essentially, a lay-off with compensation) at his factory. He'd worked there for many years and his severance package amounted to around $19,000. However, there was a two-month wait between him getting the money and the court date, so in between, he claimed to have spent it all. He told the judge that he no longer had a job *or* money.

He felt self-satisfied.

He thought he wouldn't have to pay.

He thought wrong.

The judge asked to see his superannuation papers, and after looking at them, she ruled that the amount owed would be transferred from his superannuation (pension) into mine—and not just for $10,000, but for a total of $15,000!

Once again, justice prevailed.

I got my money, but more than that, I got my total self-confidence back—the same self-confidence he had stripped from me inch by inch, day after day, for five long months.

For me, resilience had replaced obedience.

Victory had replaced venom.

Faith had replaced fear.

And just as importantly, I knew exactly what I was capable of.

I was free of Jakob.

I was free of my anger.

Mostly, I was free of my fear.

Because I confronted it.

The lioness who had been beaten into submission, taunted and terrorized, had forever broken out of her cage.

Lionesses roam free.

Eagles grace the sky.

I decided I could be both. I could be strong on land while reaching for the stars. Those stars twinkled everywhere now, and I wanted to catch their light, especially when it came to work.

I held the position of food and beverage attendant at Crown Casino for a while, but my goal was always to return to an office. The hum of photocopiers and the clicking of keyboards was like music to my ears. The conversations and meetings, the problems and solutions, were like feel-good drugs that gave me a prolonged high.

I wanted to return to the excitement, so I applied for as many jobs as I could.

Nothing was holding me back now.

I could look for whatever job *I* wanted, wherever I wanted, with whomever I wanted.

But I wasn't fussy. When I got the first job I applied for, as an administrative assistant, I grabbed it.

And when I walked through the doors on my first day, I closed my eyes and savoured the new start.

This time, I could return home smiling.

This time, I could wear whatever clothes I wanted.

This time, I wouldn't be handcuffed to someone else's paranoia.

This time, I would allow myself to truly thrive!

And very quickly, I *did* flourish.

But it was hard work.

By my own choice, I often went in to work early and left late. I was still developing my reading and writing skills in English, and the keyboard I used in Belgium was different from the one in Australia; so a task that might take someone else twenty minutes to complete took me over an hour. Add all those tasks together, and it makes for a long day and a heavy workload.

This wasn't a drawback, though. It was actually a challenge I relished.

The more English I consumed in my daily tasks, the more proficient I was becoming.

I happily worked long days and even went to the office on weekends.

Indeed, the weekends were magical. They provided a quiet haven to explore existing and new tasks. For instance, I noticed the outdated filing system was causing everyone grief. So over a few weekends and many weeknights, I redesigned and re-ordered the entire structure of the company filing. The result was that all the paperwork was readily accessible, easy to locate, and straight-forward to file again.

The clutter and confusion had gone, and in its place was a sigh of relief from everyone.

This opened the door to other processes that I could improve and streamline as well. In my view, the easier everyone's life was, the less stress we all felt, and the better we all did our jobs.

It was a win-win-win.

Or so I thought.

One day my boss, Nick, called me into his office.

I instantly wondered whether I'd overstepped my boundaries or whether my enthusiasm had bordered on annoying.

I sidled into the office and sat down, holding my breath.

Nick started saying a whole lot of words that I tried to sort through in my panicked mind. I was particularly listening for words like: 'complaints' or 'frustrating' or 'fired'. But instead, I heard: 'impressed', 'initiative', and 'appreciation'.

I let out a long exhale.

He wanted to thank me!

I was so grateful, and I told him so.

Once I realised why he wanted to speak to me, I was keen to get back to my pile of work. I was also embarrassed by the attention.

But my boss had more to say, and what he said shocked me.

'I'd like to promote you to staff liaison and public relations officer.'

Huh?

Me?

The girl who sometimes got her words mixed up?

The girl who, for months, instead of saying, 'I beg your pardon?' kept saying, 'Piggy pardon?' (Yes, that's right, PIGGY PARDON! Thankfully someone joyfully pointed out my mistake one day.)

'Err,' I said, with great eloquence, 'thank you, but I'm not sure I'm ready? There would be a lot of communication? Written, reading, and verbal, right?'

Nick smiled. 'If I didn't believe you could do it, I wouldn't offer you the promotion.'

I felt a tingling ribbon of warmth wrap around my heart. My boss believed in me more than I even believed in myself. What a gift. How fortunate I was.

'You won't be left floundering,' he reassured me. 'I understand this is a big step, and if you need to undertake any further training through online courses, the company will gladly pay for it.'

I wanted to pinch myself.

Was this a dream?

I was getting a promotion?

Further training?

Education?

His belief in me banished my own uncertainty.

I *could* make this work.

I went from nerves to enthusiasm in a matter of seconds.

I accepted the job, much to Nick's delight, and much to my own excitement.

Nick told me to investigate courses and get back to him as soon as possible.

I did just that. Over the following week I used every spare minute to research different areas of study. I explored a lot of English-speaking courses and business courses, as well as programs that included effective communication, interpersonal skills, and goal realisation.

In my searches, many customer service and communication programs appeared, but there was another course that kept cropping up too.

Life Coaching.

Life Coaching?

What in the world was a 'Life Coach?' Was it a mix between a personal trainer and a domestic duties assistant? Why did it keep appearing in my searches when it seemed so irrelevant?

After seeing it pop up over and over again, I decided to take a look.

I was totally surprised by what I read.

Life Coaching wasn't even *close* to what I imagined it to be. It was about helping people move forward with their lives by identifying obstacles, setting goals, and taking action.

Wow! It was basically the story of my own life! I could *relate* to this. From a young age, I had been blessed with the ability to identify obstacles, set goals, and take action—which is why I am now living a life of freedom.

Life Coaching would be perfect. It would be a way to help my colleagues and customers, while also improving my English.

My heart boomed.

I wanted to jump on the spot, but there wasn't time.

I kept reading.

A paragraph struck me: 'Coaching is about giving people the power to help themselves. They already know the solutions to their problems, but the answers may be obscured or difficult to acknowledge.'

Finally, there was a system of living and learning that matched my own.

One of the skills of coaching, it seemed, was knowing the right questions to ask.

Questions that would empower.

Questions that would prompt realisation and promote action.

All of a sudden, so much of my own life started to make sense.

All my life, I had been filled with questions.

I had unwittingly tormented my teachers by asking confronting questions that challenged popular belief.

I had unwittingly tormented my parents by asking confronting questions that challenged my destiny.

My enquiries were never-ending because the answers simply stirred up more questions.

Then, it dawned on me.

Maybe too many people today have stopped asking questions?
Stopped being curious?
Stopped pursuing their passion?
Stopped taking action?
Maybe they'd become dangerously comfortable with staying still?
Accepting the status quo?
Not defying their destiny?
Something else dawned on me, something I had realised long ago.
During my life, I had no one who truly understood me.

When growing up, I often felt completely alone in my curious thoughts and unusual actions. I desperately wanted for someone to understand me.

I always had a thirst for knowledge. I always wanted to know more because I always wanted to *become* more.

Little did I realise that even at the lowest points of my solitude, I was blazing my own trail and being *my own* life coach.

Everything I was reading was validating my past actions.

I *hadn't* been unreasonable or unnecessarily disruptive.

I *had* simply been navigating my own life, a life of my choosing.

All of a sudden, I felt a part of something much bigger than myself, something that encompassed my past, and would shape my future. Something that would help me to help others. Life Coaching would be my tool to create change in people, and the world.

I wanted to get started as soon as I could, so I went into work early the next morning and spoke to Nick. I explained how the Life Coaching course would be beneficial in my new role, as well as help to enhance my English. I also explained that it was a bit expensive, at $5,000.

Nick trusted my judgment and didn't care about the cost. 'It sounds excellent. Enrol as soon as you like.'

I felt profoundly humbled that he thought I was worth investing in. Consequently, I was driven to deliver.

All day I zipped around the office completing my tasks. When it was time to go, I raced home, jumped on my computer, and registered for the course.

I was almost squealing as I retrieved the modules.

I eagerly read the welcome message and the syllabus outline, and without further ado, launched into module one.

From the first paragraph, my brain was addicted, my eyes were hooked. I felt as though I was reading the most riveting book *ever* written.

My biggest challenge was slowing down. My eyes swallowed whole sentences and gulped down paragraphs, one after the other.

All the while, I was frantically scribbling notes. My papers looked like a hurricane of ink with words here, arrows there, and exclamation marks everywhere!

In the process, I found myself understanding and learning English words I'd never seen before. I could feel my vocabulary improving just through incidental learning.

My beginner's excitement did not wear off either. The euphoria continued every single night.

Every evening I devoured the course, and every day, I implemented what I learnt.

I was loving my new role at work too.

I felt like a rocket, fully fuelled, flying higher and higher.

My new life was so different from my previous life with Jakob. When I was with Jakob, the spark of my soul always tried to shine, but he extinguished it. Now, that little spark had grown into an inferno. The rising flames gave me so much energy. The fire was feeding off my past abuse. It used the cruelty as kindling.

As the flames of passion soared through my body, I was left with a burning drive.

The blaze powered me to go faster, making me more efficient and productive.

The fire danced and curled, fuelling my creativity.

The ashes of my beaten self blew away.

I felt like I was living life as a superhuman.

I'd go home, cook dinner, and eat while reading the modules. After dinner, I'd sit at the table and keep working. When it was time for bed, I'd slip under the covers and keep studying. I'd fall asleep with books clutched to my chest, and first thing in the morning, start reading them again.

I slept for only a few hours a night because I couldn't wait to open the blinds, open my books, and again open my mind.

Over the months I studied harder and harder than I thought possible.

I had to.

The course was intense.

Each module required a minimum of fifty five hours of study, though some were eighty.

I was required to do assignments, complete oral exams over the phone, and sit for practical exams in front of master coaches who watched me work with clients.

I still put in extra time at work, too, because I relished applying my study to everyday business situations.

Over the months, though, there were changes happening at work.

Departments were downsizing.

Lay-offs were being offered.

Staff were getting nervous.

Given that I had not been working there long, I was one of the first to be offered a lay-off.

But, I truly didn't mind at all. I was grateful I'd been given the opportunity to work for a boss who valued me, believed in me, and was willing to invest in my training.

Nick felt terrible about the situation, but he needn't have. Armed with a glowing reference from him, I found another job quickly. Within a fortnight I was working as a project manager for a web strategy company, enjoying the role, and continuing to savour the opportunity to put my nightly studies into daily practice.

Life continued in a rhythmic pattern of study-work-study-work for quite a while.

Eventually though, I finished the Life Coaching course. While naturally I was thrilled, I wanted to continue pursuing further education and knowledge. I especially wanted to learn specialised coaching training for corporate clients, so I invested my own money to become a Certified Business and Executive Coach.

I *loved* business. My heart belonged in business. I felt alive around business people, and I felt invigorated being one myself. I'd been around business people long enough to know their challenges, and I was eager to partner and assist.

I launched into the specialised training with vigour. The workload for this course was even heavier than for Life Coaching, but I gobbled up every module, every chance I could, and I passed all ten exams with flying colours.

In less than two years I'd gone from not knowing what Life Coaching was, to being a Certified Business and Executive Coach, all by the age of twenty-six. I felt a warm, humble sense of pride at this achievement.

I didn't want to waste valuable time though.

I decided to dive full-time into my own coaching practice.

So, in 2011, Transformations Coaching Group was born.

Transformations Coaching Group had a unique selling point. Rather than offering general coaching and helping all people with all problems, I decided to contract the best coaches in the industry who specialised in specific areas, e.g. business, relationships, fitness, public speaking, etc. This meant that, even though I was actively seeking clients for myself, if a client needed specialised coaching, I'd refer them to one of my coaching partners. It was a win-win-win situation for me, the client, and my referral partners.

I didn't just dedicate my days to coaching either.

I often invested time attending seminars and conferences in order to learn more, while simultaneously creating relationships with others.

At these events, the flow of handshakes and the exchange of information was like adrenalin pumping through one, collective body ... my body especially! My adrenaline always pumped harder at one particular point of each event though.

When the speaker was introduced.

The minute they walked on stage, I was both excited and mesmerised. I admired the way they stood up in front of everyone, seamlessly inspiring with their wisdom and stories.

I listened to them.

I watched them.

I studied them.

I even imagined what it would be like to be a speaker myself one day.

That radical thought made me catch my breath. I looked around guiltily, as though everyone had read my wild mind.

I told myself, 'Fiori, slow down, you haven't even grown your business yet! Take it one step at a time.'

So I kept stepping.

I had studied hard.

I implemented everything I'd learned from my life, as well as my formal education, into my own business.

Starting my business was like flying. The skies I once looked up to for inspiration were now the same skies in which I felt I was soaring!

I was my own boss.

I was calling the shots.

I was savouring the accountability.

I was dealing with defeats.

I was enjoying the spoils.

I dived into the sea of opportunities before me.

I networked. I reached out. I partnered with others in my field. I reconnected with those I'd met at business functions.

Then one day, I received a call.

It was from Shaun, a man I'd met at a seminar three months ago. He ran a multimillion-dollar business in Queensland.

At first I thought Shaun was calling to simply maintain our connection. But no, he was actually calling to hire me. He was having serious issues with a senior employee and wanted me to coach him through the situation.

A surge of excitement drilled into my heart, pouring truck-loads of adrenaline into it.

I was literally bouncing off the walls with exhilaration and anticipation.

'Yes, I'd be happy to coach you,' I responded, somehow staying calm.

We made arrangements over the phone, and when the call ended, I *did* bounce.

I bounced right around the apartment—leaping, dancing, singing.

When I eventually stopped to catch my breath, I reflected on the situation.

I had coached several clients already, but Shaun was my first really *big* client.

I was thrilled beyond belief.

But I was scared.

Could I really do this?

Had I made a huge mistake by accepting this job?

Surely something would go terribly wrong ...

CHAPTER NINE

TEARS AND TRANSFORMATION

The only way to let pain pass through,

is to be courageous enough to first let it in.

The voice of nerves haunted the dark halls of my mind.

They pulled down the blinds.

They smothered the light.

They whispered deep doubts.

So many doubts.

You've never coached such a big client in your life!

You can't do this.

You're going to fail.

You're too inexperienced.

You're an imposter.

Shaun is flying you to Brisbane.

He's paying all your expenses.

He's going to expect a return.

He's hired experienced coaches before.

It's going to be HUMILIATING.

And just like that, my excitement retreated into fear.

My brain became my own worst enemy.

My mind tried to sabotage my goals, and tried to undercut my hard-earned achievements. Tried to clip my wings.

Tried to.

I wouldn't let it though.

My mind wasn't a separate entity. *I* was my mind; I controlled it.

I may not be in control of all that flowed in, but I could definitely choose which thoughts to believe.

The realisation of this reminded me of a time in Belgium when hardly any employers would give me an interview. I decided to change my self-talk back then. I changed what I believed about myself. The minute I did that, I turned all the negative thoughts into positive ones, and I started getting jobs.

It was time to change my self-talk again.

I walked through those dark halls in my mind.

I switched on the lights.

I opened the windows.

Warm, fresh thoughts flowed in.

I can do this.

I've worked hard.

The only way to get experience is to do it.

Every expert was a beginner once.

It's normal to feel doubtful.

I'm nervous because I care.

I'll do my best.

I've helped others; I'll help Shaun too.

I've studied hard, and I have life experience.

The positive thoughts were instantly helpful. They strung together like sparkling strands on a chandelier.

Of course, I knew I would still have doubts, but at least I was equipped to combat them now.

Sure enough, the doubts resurfaced again as I sat on the plane to Brisbane.

'It's okay,' I reassured myself. 'You've planned for this. You even called Shaun to make sure he understood that you're inexperienced, and that you may not be successful. He told you he understood, that he'd been let down in the past by experienced coaches, and that he wanted to try someone with fresh ideas and a new approach.'

While I *should* have been reassured by the conversation with Shaun, I wasn't.

What if I let him down too?

I didn't want to be just another disappointment.

I owned my nerves. I didn't deny them, but I also didn't feed them. Negativity can be a starving beast. It can be hungry for destructive thoughts and pessimistic perspectives. I fed it positivity instead.

I can do this.

I'm nervous because I care.

I care, so I'll do my best.

The negativity struggled, unsuccessfully, to sink its teeth in, but it kept trying. It was a constant battle, but I had faith in my own chorus of optimism. That positive chorus sung to me all the way to Brisbane, and even as I travelled to my hotel.

It got quieter as I further prepared for the first meeting, and it died down completely as I took a taxi to Shaun's office. It was barely audible when I put my hand out to shake Shaun's.

But his handshake was like a lifesaver in rough seas. I could feel his confidence in me. It buoyed me. It settled my uncertainties, which was fortunate, because Shaun wanted to get down to business immediately.

Shaun took me to a boardroom, and once there, he talked at length about the issues he was having.

I listened.

I asked some questions.

I listened some more.

As Shaun spoke, in my head I was already putting pieces of the puzzle together.

I could see that some ill-fitting pieces were being forced together, while others were meshing perfectly. But my role today was about listening, not diagnosing.

At the end of the session, Shaun's demeanour seemed lighter. It's as though he'd unpacked a load of worries from his shoulders and placed them on the table for me to rake through.

And that's exactly what I did in my hotel room after the meeting.

I sorted through all the information.

I went through the notes I'd taken.

I analysed every detail.

I did some research.

I then spent hours collating and forming my ideas, and creating a plan—a plan that would be threaded together by a series of strategic questions.

I asked these questions at the second session the next day.

Shaun found some of the questions easy, the answers flying from his lips like birds to a worm.

But with others, he had to dig deep.

He had to contemplate.

He had to imagine.

He had to empathise.

In doing so, *he* came up with solutions to particular problems. *He* came up with a strategy to improve the situation. Over the course of the entire session, he skillfully identified all the brick walls in front of him.

Once he'd done that, we found ways to either break down the walls or carefully climb over them, together. We had only started this when, prior to the third session, Shaun said he was already seeing overall improvements.

I noticed that Shaun's body wasn't as tense anymore. He also looked as though he'd had his first decent sleep in a while.

My gut told me I was making a difference, and his feedback confirmed it.

In fact, his feedback was like a hand that turned down the dial on any negative noise in my head. His feedback fed my belief, and the belief became louder and greater than my doubts.

Over the course of three days, we had six fruitful and productive sessions.

At the end of my final session, Shaun said, 'You haven't just helped me with this problem; you've given me tools and strategies that I can use every single day for the rest of my life.'

I resisted the urge to do a somersault.

I felt as though the universe had hugged me.

I felt electricity sizzle through my entire system.

And as it did, a wonderful thought struck my mind like lightning.

The thought was of me as a sixteen-year-old girl, sitting across from Jamal at the restaurant in Sudan. Together we used to nut out problems and discuss the direction of the restaurant. Way back then, I remember thinking how much I enjoyed the one-on-one interactions, and how I'd love to have more in the future.

The future was here. Ten years later, that's exactly what I was doing.

All those years ago, I'd planted a tiny seed of an idea, and without realising it, gently nourished it every single day.

That tiny seed flourished into a tree, simply because I chose to plant it.

I thanked Shaun for his positive feedback, and returned to Melbourne feeling far more confident than when I'd left.

Despite the nerves and negative thoughts, I'd told myself I could do it, and I *had* done it.

Nothing could stop me now, not even my own doubts.

———⟩●⟨———

The first year of business was like a wild, wonderful garden maze filled with hedges of flowers and rows of thorns.

I always looked for ways to increase my client base and to be a better coach and business woman, but it wasn't easy. Sometimes it was exhausting and frightening, but it was *always* exhilarating, because I constantly set goals and took whatever action was needed to achieve them.

My hard work progressively paid off, as hard work generally does.

One client turned into two clients, two into four, four into eight, and in a year, I had a regular stream of people who wanted to use my services and that of my contracted coaches.

Word of mouth was working its way through parts of Melbourne, and I couldn't be happier.

The fact that I had my own corporate office premises was also thrilling. I had walked through the doors of many offices in my life, but walking through *my* office doors was almost a surreal experience. It was like walking through a barrier daily—the barrier of my destiny. It affirmed to me that absolutely anything was possible.

Anything.

Over the years I worked with dozens of executives and CEOs from a range of industries.

I felt completely honoured to partner with them to overcome challenges.

I felt humbled to witness their transformations.

Most of all, I felt blessed to see the changes not just in their business, but also their *entire* lives. Solutions flowed from the boardroom into the family room, from the office into the kitchen.

Their versions of happiness were being realised.

Their versions of purpose were being pursued, all of which added even more fuel to my skyrocketing energy.

I wanted to help more and more people, which led me to a new idea.

I was noticing a pattern of three main problems with nearly every client with whom I worked: stress; lack of clarity and direction; and feeling stuck in a rut.

Although I worked differently with each client, there were similar coaching strands in every case.

That's when I dared to dream about creating my very own coaching framework. Not a system I'd learnt about in textbooks or at lectures or from master coaches—a framework that *I'd* create based on my own knowledge and life experiences.

Could I create it?

Should I?

I dared to do it!

I threw myself into the project with gusto.

Every spare moment I had, whether in the early, hazy hours of the morning, or the late, dark hours of night, I was brainstorming and formulating.

It literally took months to create, test, refine, and implement.

But I did it; I created my framework!

My framework contained a three-step methodology that I coined 'A.R.T.'

The acronym of 'A.R.T.' stood for 'Analyse, Reframe, and Transform,' and could be used by anyone to overcome virtually any problem, gain clarity, and defy any destiny.

It worked like this ...

Through analysis, I asked specific questions that would lead to insights.

Analysis involved examining the sources of the problems by asking questions starting with 'what,' 'where,' 'when,' 'how,' 'why,' and 'who.'

For example, I had a wonderful client who was gifted with numbers. From a young age he was told by his father that he would work in the family's financial planning business, and eventually, take it over. Even as a young boy, my client understood implicitly that he'd go to university, get a degree, and work in the family business. By the time he contacted me, he was in his fifties and was a not-so-proud owner of the company. He was successful, but unfulfilled and unhappy.

My partnership with this client involved many conversations and steps, but here are the steps that relate to the A.R.T. framework.

I started by asking:

'Where is the problem you are experiencing—home, work, social setting?'

'How are you feeling?'

'When do you feel the way you're feeling?'

'What is making you feel this way?'

'Why is the situation making you feel this way?'

'Who is involved?'

'How can we improve the situation?'

His answers were telling:

'The situation is happening at work; however, the unhappiness spills over into all areas of my life, including home life and leisure time.'

'I'm feeling lost, empty, unfulfilled, stuck in a rut, demotivated, miserable.'

'At first, I would only feel this way while at work, and would perk up a bit at home and on weekends. But now, I feel demotivated most of the time.'

'My career is making me feel this way.'

'The situation is making me feel this way because my work doesn't fulfill or excite me. I don't even like working as a financial planner—I'm just good at it. I always *knew* I would work in finance. It wasn't even a conscious decision; it was just an understanding that was implanted into my head by my well-meaning father. I never thought to question or oppose his wishes. What I really enjoyed all my life was fitness. I trained a lot at the gym and read many books on fitness, but I always thought fitness had to be my side interest because job security was more important. I thought that for me, job security could only be found in finance.'

'The people involved are my father and me. Surprisingly, even though I'm a middle-aged man, I still don't want to disappoint my dad. He meant well and he was looking out for my future.'

'I can improve the situation by questioning what I really want to do with my life, and how I can work in a career that actually excites and interests me, rather than makes me feel bored and empty.'

With the answers under his belt, my client could see the problems through a new lens, which meant he was able to take the next step of *reframing his thoughts*.

His previous self-talk was: 'There's no way out. I chose this career, now I'm stuck.'

After reframing his thoughts, though, he said to himself: 'I can fix this. I can pursue a fulfilling career. I am not destined to work in finance. My father will be happiest if I am feeling fulfilled. I can help him understand, and if he doesn't understand, that's okay. It's my life, not his.'

The final step was to *transform*.

Transformation involved creating and implementing an action plan. To do this, he answered the following questions, 'What type of work will fulfil and excite me? What action can I take to secure this type of work?'

The best part about this step is that transformation occurs even *before* the plan is put into place. Just the act of *having an effective plan* sets the wheels of transformation in motion.

Over a period of about a year, my client took a number of exciting steps to gradually change his life. He sold his financial planning business but negotiated to work part-time as a consultant, meaning he was still earning a regular income, albeit a much smaller one. Then, he purchased a gym, which he recruited other staff to manage. This gym became his absolute pride and joy! He treasured both his employees and members, and his eyes would light up when he talked about both. He even got involved in programs where members could run five or ten kilometres to raise money for charity. He loved creating a sense of community.

Over the years, he went on to own a number of gyms. He defied his destiny because he wanted more fulfilment and happiness—not more money (though his gyms became highly profitable). He transformed from a man coasting along in life, to a man living with purpose, passion, and energy.

The A.R.T. framework can be used by anyone who wants to gain clarity or overcome problems. It just requires everyone to *question their situation* and *take steps to change it*, using the framework as a guide.

As soon as I started implementing the A.R.T. framework in my business, I noticed my own coaching style become more stream-lined and efficient. My clients were responding exceptionally well to it too.

I saw stressed managers become flourishing executives.
I saw the sparkle in smiles.
I saw the straightness in spines.
I saw destinies being defied.
But there's one thing I didn't see.
The sliver of emptiness quivering inside *my* soul.

———————>●<———————

Strangely, the more peace I saw in others, the less peace I experienced within myself.

Clearly, it was time to coach myself.

The way I saw it, there were a number of steps to take.

The first step was to read.

And I mean, *read*.

I devoured countless books.

Through books, all of a sudden I didn't just have my own insight, I had the insight of two people, three people, four people ... fifty people.

The different viewpoints were invaluable in helping me make well-informed daily choices, as well as big life decisions.

I certainly didn't believe every piece of information from every single book, but I took ribbons of colour and wisdom from each, creating my own personal rainbow. Every devoured book created another layer of rich soil in my subconscious mind, providing fresh, fertile ground for my own ideas to grow.

Reading ... ticked off!

The second step in my transformation journey involved releasing pain.

As a result of growing up in a war-torn country, I'd witnessed unspeakable physical, emotional, and psychological cruelty, all from a young age. Many of the acts I witnessed were so gruesome and brutal that I locked them deep in a cave within my soul. But we all know what happens in caves, especially in horror movies: bats come blurting out at the worst possible time.

I decided I needed to clear out the cave, on my terms. I needed to set the bats free, in my own timing.

Although difficult sometimes, I spoke to trusted and empathetic people who listened without judgement to my traumatic stories. These people didn't provide solutions or deliver platitudes, like, 'Look on the bright side ...'

I *knew* life had a bright side. I was living on that side with the sun bathing my face. But noticing the light doesn't get rid of the dark. Embracing the dark *leads* to the light.

The people I confided in never minimised my experiences in any way. Their simple yet profound act of listening helped me release the bats.

I instantly felt lighter. Even *more* free.

That additional sense of freedom was cause to be grateful.

And indeed, gratefulness was a part of my transformation journey as well—the third important step.

I had always been grateful for important aspects of my life, but my busyness smothered the gratefulness I felt for everyday blessings.

I changed that.

Gratefulness became a stream of mini, moment-to-moment prayers. They were bite-sized jewels of appreciation that sparkled from every cell in my body. Gratefulness became one, long song that played in my head from the moment I woke up to the moment I went to bed.

Thank you for the gift of waking up. It means I'm alive and well.

Thank you for running water.

Thank you for this hot shower.

Thank you for my functioning legs, arms, and mind.

Thank you for the scowling driver—he helped me value friendliness and taught me patience.

Thank you for Jenny calling, even at my busiest time—I am lucky to have wonderful friends.

Everything, no matter how big or small, I became mindfully grateful for.

Feeling grateful helped me to be more generous, more empathetic, more loving, more *full*. I never felt empty, jealous, or resentful when I practiced gratefulness. I just felt bliss.

Gratefulness created a steel-like force field around me that helped to deflect everyday annoyances, while encouraging me to maintain perspective and positivity.

Needless to say, I was grateful for gratefulness!

The fourth step on my road to transformation was exercise.

Even though I loved exercise, it was often the first activity I cut from my day to get more tasks done. But where I gained time, I lost the priceless health and mental benefits of moving my body and increasing my heart rate.

To ensure I didn't fall into the pattern of not prioritising exercise, I hired a personal trainer. He was a lovely person who I enjoyed bantering with, but the fact that I had to pay him monthly (whether or not I used his services!) gave me the push I needed to exercise consistently again.

When I exercised, my heart imitated the thumping, pounding rhythm of African drumbeats.

It was like a dance.

I gave myself willingly to that dance, day in and day out.

Stress fizzled away, and joy flooded in.

I breathed hard, like a dragon. I felt invincible after exercise. It gave me energy, clarity, motivation, and confidence.

And with more energy, I had more emotional reserves to focus on the fifth step in my transformation journey: making a contribution.

I had always seen myself as a kind person, but the kindness I wanted to focus on more was through generosity and giving.

Growing up, I watched my parents give a percentage of their earnings to the church, and another percentage to the poor in our neighbourhood.

That sense of giving definitely was passed down to me, and sometimes it also got me into trouble! When I was managing my parents' grocery store at such a young age, I loved the smiles on the villagers' faces when I gave them food and items for free. At the end of the day, I was so excited to tell my parents about all the stock I'd donated! They didn't quite share my joy. They'd say, 'The stock is not yours to give away, it's ours. Your job is to sell, not donate. We'll do the giving, you do the selling.'

I couldn't stop, though. I kept giving stuff away, I just didn't tell my parents about it anymore! Even though they would have known, they turned a blind eye. Deep down I think they were proud I was empathetic.

When I moved to other countries, I continued my habit by donating to non-profit organisations. I also cooked meals for the homeless and delivered blankets and clothes, especially during holiday seasons. But since starting my business, I'd dropped the ball. That lack of giving quickly led to a sense of emptiness.

During my transformation process, as a symbol of my recommitment to the habit of giving, I decided to do something a bit different. I decided I would run a half marathon. This would serve two purposes: first, it would help me raise money for a charity; and second, the daily training would reinforce my giving habit— because every day as I pulled on my sneakers, I'd remember *why* I was training.

The charity I chose was the JMB Foundation, which is a Victorian foundation set up for and in honour of James Macready-

Bryan who sustained an acquired brain injury after being sense-lessly assaulted on his twentieth birthday.

The foundation provided financial support for the care and rehabilitation of James, as well as other sufferers. It gave a public voice to those suffering, including their families. I felt a kinship to this charity because in my lifetime, I had often battled to have my voice heard. I was keen to give a voice to those who, tragically, were given a destiny not of their choosing.

I encouraged my friends and family to donate to the foundation, and I doubled my initially promised funds. I completed the twenty-one kilometre marathon, and I re-estab-lished my habit of giving!

As an aside, I've noticed that whenever I give to others from a place of pure kindness, I gain something in return. Sometimes I enjoy good karma. Sometimes I achieve a slice of success. But most of all, I always feel *really* fantastic! Earning money is good, but giving it away to those in need is *great*. Of course, the act of receiving is not a reason to give or to be kind. It's just a natural, automatic gift from the universe.

The sixth step in my journey involved getting rid of material possessions that were bought with the wrong intention.

I love earning money. I love giving. I love buying meaningful things.

However, on a rummage through some stored items, I remembered a time when my beliefs about possessions were quite different. Stored away were expensive items I'd bought years ago—

like ski gear, furniture, sporting equipment, and more—at a time when I thought material possessions would make me happy, rather than serve a practical or fun purpose. In fact, I had bought most items because I'd seen them being worn or used by someone who looked happy. I thought that if I wore or used the same thing, that I too would be happy. Not surprisingly, the items hadn't brought me joy, which is why many of them were barely used, if at all.

They had become physical and emotional clutter.

They had to go.

As part of my transformation journey I gave these items away, which created some much-needed, refreshing and revitalising space.

What I know now, which wasn't evident to me then, is that happiness is achieved through purpose, drive, goals, fulfilment, gratitude, giving, self-love, and self-forgiveness—not material possessions that are bought to fill an emotional void.

The seventh step in my journey, again, involved creating space, but of a different kind.

It was a big step.

A difficult step.

It involved distancing myself from negative or unkind people.

There's a proverb: 'Tell me with whom you walk and I will tell you who you are.'

Research supports this proverb, because apparently we are the sum total of the top five people we spend the most time with. This means if the people around us (family, friends, partners, clients, colleagues) are positive and uplifting, so are we. If they're the opposite, sadly, so are we.

At times, I felt there were people around me who didn't have my best interests at heart, as I did theirs. But I had fallen into the trap of coasting along and settling, rather than doing something about it. *Settling* is the enemy of defying one's destiny; yet, that's exactly what I was doing with some of my relationships.

During this transformation step, I reflected on conversations I'd had with others. I remembered people bragging about their friendships that spanned decades. The length of a friendship did not impress, because to me, time and familiarity are not the markers of a thriving, positive friendship. To me the markers are empathy, inspiration, support, trust, integrity, and mutual values.

I realised it was time to take action.

I decided that anyone who wasn't nourishing my soul—either as a result of their jealousy, insecurity, paranoia, unkindness, impatience, or any other reason—no longer had a place in my life.

Thankfully, I didn't have to cut anyone out of my life in a formal or hurtful way. I just eased myself out of contact with them.

When I detoxed my life of these negative relationships, it made an immediate impact. I felt as though the grey clouds hanging over me had been blown away by a refreshing, warm breeze. That breeze blew in *new* relationships that were uplifting and positive.

There were more steps to take though.

Believe it or not, public speaking was the eighth vital step in my transformation journey.

I feel that sharing a message publicly taps into a force that is much greater than all of us.

For me, public speaking helps me share light, love, and whatever wisdom I have been fortunate to gain from others, to all those around me—which is why I wanted it to be an active part of my life. As a child, I would spontaneously stand up and speak, unafraid. But as I grew older and associated with people who cut me down—like my ex-husband—I became more self-conscious and nervous about sharing my views on a public platform.

As terrifying as it was, I pushed through the nerves and began public speaking again. With English not being my first language, I had to work harder than the average person to speak publicly, and in fact, I still do! Back then, though, I went to Toastmasters and soaked up every bit of advice they had to offer.

I remember the first time I spoke in front of my Toastmasters group ... not my best day! I went completely blank and fumbled my way through the entire presentation.

But I persisted, that day, and every other day after that. Through practice, preparation and perseverance, I ended up delivering over forty Toastmaster presentations, and surprisingly, even winning an award. Nowadays I speak to non-profit organisations, schools, the corporate sector, charity groups, industry associations, and more.

When someone speaks to me after a presentation, or emails me when they get back to their home or office to convey their feedback, I feel totally thrilled. To know that my words have possibly changed the course of their lives is the greatest honour.

The ninth step in my transformation journey involved saying affirmations.

An affirmation is a declaration, validation, or confirmation of a statement that we believe to be true, like, 'I can do it.' By saying positive affirmations, I was taking conscious control of my thoughts.

Throughout my life I had used affirmations on and off, but as part of my transformation journey, I said them throughout the day. Affirmations became one of the most powerful techniques for creating profound and sustainable changes in my life. In fact, affirmations made such an impact on me that, based on my research and personal journey with them, I created my very own affirmations on thirty different subjects. My mind had become a positive valley, and I wanted others to join me there.

Also highly beneficial was meditation, and it was the tenth important step for me.

In the past, I used to meditate without fail. When I did, it set a peaceful tone for my entire day. No matter what the world threw at me, I could handle it. I could get a parking ticket or be verbally abused by a rude person, but with meditation under my belt, I would stay calm and simply focus on the solutions. Without meditation, I focused on the problem, leading to stress and frustration.

Lately, I'd lost the habit of meditating and I *had* to get it back, because I craved the stream of serenity that eased me through the day.

But returning to meditation was much harder than expected.

Running the business, my days were jam-packed with meetings and a heavy workload. When I sat down to meditate, my thoughts were like a million gymnasts doing their routines on the shifting floors of my hyperactive mind. My thoughts twisted and turned, tumbled and rumbled, flipped and flew.

At times, meditation seemed impossible, with a perpetual tug-of-war between expectation and reality. A battleground with one side launching weapons, while the other side yelled, 'QUIET!'

But I didn't give up. I knew that meditation was like a muscle. If I stopped, it would weaken; if I used it regularly, it would strengthen.

So I did more reading and research.

I immersed myself in books and videos.

I read and watched. Read and watched.

Over time, I realised something both comforting and clarifying.

Meditation was different for everyone, and as such, could be practiced *differently* by everyone.

For me, it didn't have to be about stilling the mind by attempting to rid my mind of all thoughts. Sometimes, it could simply be about stilling the mind through focusing on *one* thought.

The *focus* rather than the *emptiness* created peace and stillness.

By focusing on one thought, *I* was in control. I was taking my mind to where *I* wanted it to go. I was being mindful, rather than mind-*less*. By focusing on one thought, I was staying in the moment.

So that's what I did—I stayed in the moment.

I would focus on repeating a word or a positive affirmation.

I would practice gratefulness.

I would focus on my breath, thinking 'nourishment for mind and body' on the inhalation, and 'stress release is detoxing' on the exhalation.

I would mindfully sweep the floor, mindfully do the dishes, mindfully walk down a busy street.

But mostly, I enjoyed sitting in one spot, focusing on one ... simple ... thought.

In time, the benefits flowed in. My focus and concentration stayed sharper for longer. I felt a sense of clarity. My overall outlook on life improved as I focused on abundance, love, and grace, rather than scarcity and negativity.

Meditation gave me the stillness to reach out and truly heal. It was the chalice that held my empathy. It was the observation tower that gave me a 360 degree view of every situation. And surprisingly, it's the place I experienced the most profound, confronting, and life-changing moment in my transformation journey.

This is what happened.

———————⟫●⟪———————

One day while in a meditative state, a thought flowed in.

This thought soaked my mind, leaving it to drip heavily. It's a thought that had washed in several times. A thought so disturbing, it always prompted me to stop meditating.

This time, though, I didn't stop.

I accepted the thought, embraced my reaction, and faced my fear.

The thought, or vision, was of beautiful Amanuel.

He was waving from a boat, calling to me.

I gulped in the air, taking in extra for Amanuel.

I felt a suffocating sense of grief.

I felt an unbearable sense of loss.

I felt an overpowering sense of guilt. A guilt so heavy, it weighed down on each shoulder like an anchor.

I hadn't protected him.

I hadn't saved him.

There he was.

My brother.

My beautiful brother.

His smile almost reached both ends of the world.

With my eyes closed, I brought Amanuel into the room so I could connect with him spiritually.

In my mind's eye, he sat opposite me, cross-legged.

He liked this activity. He was grinning.

Growing up, we shared an umbilical cord that connected and fed both our minds. We knew what each other was thinking. We'd finish each other's sentences.

Because of this connection, it was time to have a conversation with Amanuel. I would let what I *thought* he'd say flow into my mind, and I'd reply. Together, we'd find a way through this painful puzzle of guilt and loss.

'I miss you Amanuel,' I told him. 'I miss not being able to talk to you, to hold you, to protect you.'

He smiled. 'I don't miss you, Fiori, because I am always with you. I am with you as you walk, talk, and live. Every time you think of me, which I know is often, you are holding me in your heart, protecting me still.'

'I'm so sorry, Amanuel.'

Tears began puddling in my eyes.

I let them.

I let my mind and body say and do whatever it needed to.

'What for?' he asked. 'You've done nothing wrong.'

'I pushed you out of your comfort zone. I kept telling you to leave Libya, to get on the boat.'

'And why did you encourage me to leave Libya, Fiori?'

'Because you were suffering in Libya.'

'In what way was I suffering?' he asked.

'You were being beaten, stolen from, fleeced by scammers. You were being thrown into prison, needing to bribe your way out. I kept sending you money to keep you safe. I didn't care about the money. The money wasn't important—your safety was. I was scared for you. I missed you. I wanted you here.'

'Exactly,' he said, smiling. 'In explaining it to me, I hope you've also explained it to yourself?'

'Explained what?'

'You love me, Fiori. You have always protected me. You wanted to help me. Everything you said and did came from a place of the purest love.'

'I feel so guilty,' I confessed, sobbing now.

'Let me ask you then. Did you *want* my boat to leak, Fiori?'

'No!'

'Did you want me to go missing?'

'Of course not!'

'Did you try to do something when the boat went missing?'

'Yes, I tried *everything*. I called everyone. And I didn't *stop* calling.'

'Would you have encouraged me to get on the boat if you knew it wasn't seaworthy?'

'NO!'

'If you knew it wasn't seaworthy, what would you have said to me?'

'I would have told you to stay in Libya for the rest of your life, or return to Sudan, or even go back to Eritrea! I would have done everything in my power to stop you from getting on that boat.'

'Sweet Fiori, don't you see? *Can't* you see?'

I stopped.

My mouth fell open.

I listened.

I sobbed.

'You do finally see,' he said. '*It wasn't your fault.*'

I put my head in my hands and let the tears drench them.

'You are not to blame,' he continued. 'You cannot hold yourself responsible forever. What happened was God's plan. Or, as you would say, the universe's plan. Both are right, Fiori. God *is* the universe. It was *meant* to happen, even if you will never know the reason why. It was my destiny. I couldn't defy it.'

His last words triggered me to stop crying.

'Yes,' he said, laughing. 'You are teaching everyone to defy their destiny, but I couldn't defy my own. That must be hard for you. Tell me, Fiori, do you feel you are finally defying *your* destiny?'

'Yes, of course,' I whispered.

'Really? Are you sure? Your destiny is to keep pursuing freedom, for yourself and others. But will you feel true freedom if you are always a slave to your guilt?'

The time for big sister lecturing was over.

My brother was talking.

It was my turn to listen.

'If guilt is eating away at you, Fiori, it's eating away at me too. I am miserable, if you are. On the other hand, I am happy if you are. We can do so much good in the world, you and I, if you let us. All my life, you have guided me. Now, let me be your guide.'

I sat very still.

I listened.

'Fiori, I am no longer missing at sea. I have been found, safe and well, in your heart. Accept that fact, and allow me to protect you, guide you, love you. Let go of what you can't control, and you'll finally be free. There is great freedom in self-forgiveness.'

I fluttered my eyes open after his last sentence. I don't know why.

The conversation ended there.

Maybe I ended it.

Maybe Amanuel did.

But it was over, for then.

My entire face was soaked with tears, but I felt surprisingly light and refreshed. I felt as though the anchors hooked over each shoulder had been lifted, and in their place were wings. The wings of an eagle.

The eagle that once stirred inside me, I had now *become.*

From that day forward, I soared without the weight of guilt dragging me to the bottom of a stormy ocean.

I knew that Amanuel was looking out for me.

I had many more conversations with Amanuel after that first one, and I continue to do so to this very day. I seek his wise counsel when needed, and share both my good and bad news with him.

I never feel alone. He's beside me as I fight for injustices. As I share my story. As I create *new* stories. Nothing is more real in my life than Amanuel's presence in it.

I still have pangs of guilt in low moments, but it's fleeting now. I forgave myself that day. And through true self-forgiveness came true freedom. It was the final step in my transformation journey.

It's important to note that the word 'journey' is definitely the operative word. Just because I undertook the journey doesn't mean I made a final transformation.

For me, transformation has been, and always *will* be, like a deciduous tree—sometimes flourishing, sometimes losing its leaves.

At the time of working on this book, my life partner, Ben, and I have a newborn baby, and most days I'm working between the hours of 2:30 a.m. and 7:00 a.m. The rest of the day is a blur of blissful baby and family time, answering emails, speaking at events, attending meetings, having friends and family over, and more.

Right now, I'm doing my best. Some days I meditate; other days I don't. Some days I'm grateful; other days I'm not. Some days I'll exercise; other days I'll nap.

One thing is for sure ... whenever I neglect some or all of the transformation steps, I start to feel empty and unhappy, so I am drawn back to them.

I know that throughout my life, I will slip in and out of these good transformation habits. But I will always return, because every moment that I actively transform is a *defining* moment.

I have had many defining moments in my life, several of which I've already shared.

But, there are others I must tell you about. Some good. Some very bad.

All of them helping me to defy my destiny.

DEFINING MOMENTS

When you take just one step toward defying

your destiny, the size of the step is irrelevant—

the decision to make it, is enormous.

T he truth is, nearly every moment in my life has been defining in one way or another, but some moments have taught me specific, standout lessons.

These lessons are part of bigger stories.

I'm going to share five of these stories, five of these defining moments.

A JOB OFFER WITH A DIFFERENCE

When I was in Belgium, I did some part-time modelling work for a young fashion designer.

The designer's name was Danny, and he'd created a small, stylish clothing line.

I'd wear his clothes and he'd photograph me for brochures and advertisements, or sometimes just use me as a fitting model.

Over time I got to know Danny quite well. He always praised my drive and often looked for opportunities for me, which I really appreciated.

One day, Danny told me about a client, James, for whom he made custom suits.

Danny said it would be beneficial to meet James because he had many contacts in the modelling industry. Also, as a successful business man, James might have a suitable position for me in one of his companies.

I happily accepted Danny's kind offer because I understood the worth of building relationships and making connections.

A few days later I met James at a restaurant.

I spotted him immediately. He was around sixty years old and had a lovely mane of silvery hair and clear, olive skin.

When I arrived at the table, James stood up and shook my hand. 'I've heard a lot of about you, Fiori. I'm looking forward to finding out more.'

'Thank you,' I said. 'I've heard a lot about you too.'

'Good, let's get to it.'

James proceeded to ask a lot of questions about my plans for the future, my hopes and dreams. He was businesslike, but polite. He looked me square in the eyes in a way that suggested he was focused and interested.

I told him I enjoyed part-time modelling, but that I also enjoyed different types of work. I outlined my typing speed and administration capabilities, as well as my strong work ethic. I asked if these were the sort of attributes he was looking for.

James nodded. 'Yes, they are. Look, I have contacts with a number of big modelling agencies, but after listening to you, I think you'd be better suited to a job I have in a new company I'm starting. The job isn't necessarily a difficult one, but it requires determination and the ability to learn. I can see you have both these attributes.'

I eagerly leant forward. 'Thank you.'

He explained the role to me. It involved training a team to sell a new line of hospital equipment.

Me?

Train a sales team?

I nodded along professionally while my insides started doing excited, rampant cartwheels.

James spoke for a while longer, and when the meeting wrapped up, he said, 'Let's take it one step at a time. Send me some modelling portfolio pictures which I can show agencies, as well as a letter explaining why you'd be suited for the sales trainer position.'

Cartwheels.

More cartwheels.

I smiled, shook his hand, and when I was out of his sight, pumped my fists in celebration.

I got back home, and as soon as I could, sent James some of my best portfolio photographs. I also sent my updated resume that I'd tweaked and tailored specifically for the sales position.

From there, I waited and hoped.

James' assistant, Sharon, called me in a matter of days to let me know I'd been selected for an interview.

I was so excited!

She also told me that the interview was in Dublin, as was the job. I hadn't been aware of the job location, but it didn't matter. I'd interviewed for other overseas positions and was willing to relocate for the right one.

Sharon took my details and said she'd make all the arrangements.

That she did, very quickly.

She sent me details of the flight, and before I knew it, I was on the plane, off the plane, and standing in James' offices in Dublin.

Sharon showed me around the building. She explained that James was in a meeting but that he'd like to meet me for lunch at a restaurant.

James' driver, who had previously picked me up from the airport, took me to meet James. He drove to a part of Dublin that seemed prestigious and fancy, because the restaurant was nestled amidst a strip of upmarket clothing stores.

I sat in the restaurant, pinching myself at how fortunate I was to get an interview.

When twenty minutes passed, though, I wondered whether James was going to show up at all.

Just at that moment, the driver walked in.

'James is still in his meeting,' he said, 'but he asked me to extend his apologies for keeping you waiting. Instead, he'll meet you for dinner tonight at your hotel restaurant. Please meet him at eight.'

'No need to apologise,' I said, well aware of how meetings can run over. 'I'll see him later.'

'James asked me to pass along this gift,' the driver said, 'so you can at least enjoy an afternoon of shopping.'

The gift referred to a huge wad of cash. There must have been hundreds, if not thousands, of dollars in the bundle.

I immediately shook my head and put my hand up like a stop sign. 'I really appreciate the offer, but I won't accept it. I'll go shopping with my own money, but thanks anyway.'

'Are you sure?' he asked, puzzled.

'Yes, very sure,' I replied.

There's no way I could have accepted such a lavish gift.

I left the restaurant and browsed through some of the stores on my own, but quickly realised I couldn't afford anything. No problem, though. I walked back to where James was waiting and requested that he please drive me back to my hotel, which he happily did.

That night I put on a dress I'd brought from Belgium. It wasn't a fancy dress from an expensive store, but it was extra beautiful to me because it was mine, bought with my money.

I went downstairs and was surprised to see James already sitting at a table.

He extended his hand warmly. 'I'm sorry about this afternoon.'

I waved away his apology. 'It's no problem. I just appreciate the opportunity to be here.'

Given our loss of time earlier, and how busy James was, I assumed he'd want to commence business discussions fairly soon, but instead, he engaged in a lot of small talk and light-hearted conversation.

He seemed quite relaxed at the end of a hard day, and I saw a funny, charismatic side to him. There was a lot of humorous banter and laughter.

'Okay Fiori,' he said, 'we're going to talk about the job position soon, but first, I have some exciting news!'

'Great, what is it?'

'In six months' time, in July, I'm getting married.'

'Congratulations!' I said. 'I'm happy for you! Who is the lucky lady?'

He shrugged. 'I don't know yet.'

I laughed.

He didn't laugh back. In fact, he looked at me rather intently.

'Sorry James, I don't understand?'

'Well, this is where you come in, Fiori. I'd be honoured if *you* would be my wife.'

My jaw nearly plummeted into my chicken soup.

'Pardon?'

He smiled. 'Let me explain. I think you are a beautiful and fascinating young woman. You're also smart and driven. I'd really love someone like you as my wife. I mean, I realise there's an age difference.'

I did the calculation in my head. Around forty years.

'But, I will make you a very happy woman, Fiori. You'll have the best of everything. The finest jewellery, glamourous clothes, a beautiful home with me. You can have nearly everything your heart desires.'

My forehead crinkled as I tried to process all the information.

'But not kids,' he continued. 'I can't have kids because I already have two grown children who are twenty-eight and twenty-three. And, I know that you're twenty-one.'

So I was younger than his youngest daughter?

'My only condition is that you can't pursue your career as a model or corporate employee. You really can't work at all, but that shouldn't be a problem because you'll have everything you want. You won't need to work.'

At this point, I realised the whole thing must be a big joke. James would soon burst out laughing, just as he'd done previously after another funny story.

I giggled nervously. 'I'm just waiting for the punchline, James!'

He smirked but shook his head. 'This definitely isn't a joke. In fact, it's a serious, once-in-a-lifetime opportunity for you. I know plenty of women who would do anything for an opportunity like this, but I'm choosing you because you remind me of a younger version of myself.'

If I *really* reminded James of a younger version of himself, I wondered why he would want to suppress my dreams and smother my ambition?

And yet, on another level, I understood.

I understood that he may want a young wife. I understood that it would give him enormous joy to spoil and provide for an appreciative, energetic, young woman. I also understood that any number of smart, wonderful women would adore that life, and happily accept that offer.

I just wasn't one of those women.

Without the ability to work and have a career, I would be a tree without water. Delicious meals and beautiful dresses wouldn't nourish or feed me. No mansion would be big enough to contain my sadness.

Added to all that, I wasn't attracted to James, and I definitely didn't love him, given I'd only just met him!

'It's a lot to take in,' he said, studying me.

I stretched a smile across my face. 'Thank you for the offer, but my career is important to me. You said I remind you of yourself, so I'm sure you understand why I can't accept.'

For a moment he said nothing, but then he shrugged, as though my words meant nothing to him. 'That's fine. No hard feelings. I personally think you're making a huge mistake, but I respect your decision.'

'Thank you James.'

His tone became businesslike. 'Visit the office again tomorrow and keep learning about our new business, and we'll see if you're suitable for the position.'

While I was relieved that the offer was still on the table, James' tone was certainly more sterile and formal. Even if I did get the job, I wasn't sure whether it would be wise to accept it.

The next morning I called James' assistant, Sharon, and asked her to please send the driver to take me to the office, which was always the plan. Not surprisingly, she told me the driver was busy and I'd have to make my own way.

I smiled.

I should have expected that.

It wasn't an issue, however, because making my own way was my *favourite* way.

I took a taxi, and once at the offices I attended some meetings, spoke to a few people, and that afternoon, was offered the job.

After the previous night's conversation with James, though, I decided to decline. I told James it was because I didn't want to move to Dublin, but the real reason was because my intuition told me not to.

I love my intuition.

It's a gift nuzzled deep in my gut, wrapped in glistening paper and tied with sparkling bows. It contains the most priceless gift of all: the *answer*.

The way forward.

The right path.

The better option.

Accepting the position was right on every level for my career.

But my gut shook its head and said: *No. Just no.*

Any time I've ignored my intuition (and I have several times!), I've paid for it in one way or another. I wasn't going to pay for this mistake too.

There were no hard feelings between James and me. He filled his position quickly, and I have no doubt he found a suitable wife.

I classify this experience with James as a 'defining moment,' because it was yet another crucial point in my life where I defied my destiny.

I could have taken the path that wasn't true to my heart.

I could have married a rich man and wanted for nothing.

But I would have paid dearly. I would have ended up a zombie, alive on the outside but completely dead on the inside.

I sometimes wonder how different my life would have been if I didn't defy that particular destiny.

How lost I'd be.

How empty I would feel.

My destiny, everyone's destiny, is challenged every single day.

Our moment-to-moment decisions define or *defy* our destinies.

Perhaps we're tempted to send a text message while driving?

Enjoy that forbidden kiss?

Eat an entire pizza rather than a couple of slices?

Stop doing exercise?

Stay at that hated job?

Ingest that drug?

Destiny is our path up an unending mountain. A mountain dotted with mini summits, where the view is either bright or brutal, depending on the twists and turns we've taken.

Destiny isn't just about defying the big, looming default plans— like escaping from being a child bride or a child soldier. It's about resisting and refusing the everyday destinies that lure us from our true path, our true purpose, our true passions.

Sometimes those destinies can tantalise and tease. They can dance provocatively in front of us, tempting us with their beauty. They can embrace us into their clouds of white, only to consume us later with their darkest thunder.

No matter where we've ended up, if we keep putting one foot in front of the other, there is always another summit where we can redefine, reset, refresh, and restart.

Every day is a new opportunity to start over again.

Choices, accountability, and action will take us to wherever we want to go.

POWER AND CONTROL

I will always be grateful for my life lessons and defining moments, good and bad.

But I admit, some have been harder to be grateful for, including the ones involving sexual harassment.

When I worked as a dishwasher at the Spanish restaurant in Belgium, there was a chef with dark intentions.

Sometimes he'd rub himself against me.

Sometimes he'd touch my backside.

Sometimes he'd brush against my breasts.

I'd say 'stop' or 'back off,' but he'd just casually reply with, 'Sorry, it was an accident.' Within hours the same 'accident' would happen again.

Every time he invaded my personal space in that sick way, I felt angry and completely violated. His actions unzipped the outer layer of who I was, removing my personality and rendering me nothing but a body.

A piece of meat.

A play thing for his pleasure.

As well as feeling violated, I also felt a thick layer of shame.

Was I inviting this?

Was my t-shirt a bit too tight?

Were my jeans too hugging?

Did I smile in a way that was suggestive?

I hated thinking it was my fault, and yet, I couldn't help it.

I tried avoiding the chef as much as possible. As he walked past, I'd strategically put my back against the wall. I'd curl into myself. Or I'd leave the space altogether.

But it wasn't always possible. The kitchen was small and busy, the perfect place for imperfect intentions.

Eventually, I couldn't take it any longer. I put the shame aside. It *wasn't* my fault. I went to my boss and told him what was happening. He listened carefully and nodded, but didn't seem overly concerned, or even surprised. But he promised to talk to the chef.

After a week there was no change, so I told my boss again.

Again, he said he'd speak to him.

After another week, I returned to my boss, this time agitated and upset. He looked at me apologetically and said, 'I believe what you're saying, Fiori, but I've spoken to him. If he hasn't stopped, there isn't much I can do about it. There are only a few good

Spanish chefs in Antwerp. I'm sorry, but I need him more than I need you. I understand if you want to quit.'

A film of tears glazed my eyes.

I was losing my job because of someone else's wrongdoing.

That was wrong.

I had worked hard.

I was punctual.

Reliable.

Committed.

Professional.

I treated my job with the respect it deserved, despite *just* being a dishwasher.

Having to quit was one of the most disheartening moments of my life, but I didn't let my boss see me cry.

I removed my apron and walked out with my head held high.

That was the end of that job, but not the end of my exposure to sexual harassment.

Sexual harassment seemed to follow me everywhere. Actually, it had happened before the restaurant incident, and did for a long time after.

Sometimes I felt as though I had a sign on my back that read: 'Harass me! Use me!'

Many men I have worked for in various jobs have wrongly assumed I'd love to sleep with them. They'd buy me gifts, offer me money, or promise me work opportunities—all with the understanding that sex was part of the transaction. When I'd instantly refuse their advances or propositions, they would either be insulted or angry.

The end result was always the same.

I was fired, or forced to quit.

I trudged out of so many jobs, my heart sinking with sadness and bursting with madness.

I worked my fingers to the bone in every single job. My only crime was standing up for myself, and for what was right.

I felt so much anger toward those men, not just on my behalf, but on behalf of all the other females who I knew were also being harassed. I'd hear stories of what was happening in workplaces, at social gatherings, and out on the street. Some women talked about it; many didn't. They didn't think anyone would listen or care. Many felt they'd be blamed, because deep down they felt responsible.

For me, those uncomfortable experiences, those defining moments (along with later life experiences involving Jakob), have given me a greater sense of self-respect, resolve, empowerment, and self-reliance.

Yes, my body is a piece of flesh, but that flesh wraps around a fiery heart, an active mind, and a spear-like spine.

No one will think they have the right to harass or intimidate me again, unless I let them.

And believe me—I won't.

A BLACK GIRL IN THE WRONG SUBURB

I lived in Melbourne's Docklands for two years.

During that time, I joined a popular boxing and karate gym in the city. That gym was a constant hive of activity, with over seventy different martial arts and boxing classes per week.

Some of the classes started early, with the first one kicking off at 5:30 a.m. I loved the early classes, because they set me on a positive physical and mental path for the entire day.

One morning I cycled to the gym and waited for it to open alongside the other regulars, many of whom I knew.

As I walked in, there was a receptionist I hadn't seen before.

I swiped my gym card, and as always, my personal details displayed on the screen in front of her.

The receptionist made a weird face, as though thinking: *This black woman can't live in Docklands.* (I wasn't being paranoid. I knew the face of racism. I'd seen its ugly side *many* times before.)

She stopped me and said condescendingly, 'We have the wrong address for you. Can I have the right address?'

I knew the details on the system were correct, and that her intention was to humiliate me. Still, I asked which address they had.

Sure enough, it was the Docklands' address.

'That's where I live,' I stated.

She looked at me skeptically.

I looked back at her.

She then rolled her eyes, and said, 'Fine, go on then.'

As I walked through the turnstiles, I felt as though my dignity stayed at the gate.

I felt exposed.

Raw.

Self-conscious.

I dared not look around, in case everyone was staring at me. Judging me. Questioning my honesty.

I walked into my boxing class, eyes down.

For the entire workout, I hunched into myself.

My self-consciousness turned to annoyance, as I mentally replayed the incident over and over again.

In the boxing class, our coach wanted us to spar with a partner.

But I was distracted.

Angry.

Unfocused.

I was taking hits. Moving slowly. Becoming a punching bag.

My coach kept saying, 'What's wrong with you? Where are you this morning? Why aren't you listening?'

I *was* listening, but to the wrong voice, to the angry voice in my head.

Since I performed poorly in the boxing class, I decided to stay longer at the gym to work out some more. But as I did weights, I started to sweat from fury rather than fitness. I was thinking to myself, 'The foundation of who we are is the same. Our blood is red and our bones are white. How dare she? What right does she have? No one is superior or inferior to me!'

I couldn't let go of the incident.

It plagued my entire workout.

In fact, it plagued all my workouts, because after that exchange with the receptionist, the gym never felt the same to me again. It was the place I felt crushed rather than empowered.

But I'd felt crushed *many* times in my life as a result of racism. Like, when I was followed around by security guards or sales assistants who thought I was going to steal from their store.

Like, when I'd been pulled over by police for no apparent reason.

Like, when people mockingly asked me questions, such as, 'When you were in Africa, did you drink from a dirty river?' Or, 'If you're from Africa, why do you have a normal nose?' (In other words, why wasn't my nose flat, like the media's stereotypical image of Africans?)

I have felt crushed many times, but for some reason, the gym incident bothered me a *lot*.

Maybe it was a cumulative annoyance. Maybe after so many racist comments and incidents, I had reached a point where I'd had enough.

The racism at the gym that day was the tipping point. A point where racism was either going to make me or break me.

It was a defining moment because I was faced with two roads, two destinies. This had happened once before, in Belgium.

Back then, as now, I could either allow racism to consume me, or use it to empower me.

I chose empowerment.

I chose to understand.

To empathise.

And the moment I did, racism became a gift rather than a grievance.

The incident at the gym, and all the others that preceded it, taught me about the complex, cratered surface of racism.

I realised that racism is not about *me* at all.

It's about the person who perpetrates it.

A person's racism is a result of their own fears, experiences, intolerances, and insecurities, which all mostly stem from their upbringing. While some people develop prejudices later in life, most of the time, it has been passed down by parents and other role models.

I felt sad that such misguided beliefs could trickle down through generations, unquestioned.

I felt disappointed that many people allowed their destiny to be plagued by racist beliefs.

But I felt glad too. I'd shifted from anger to understanding, and that anger could have held me back my entire life.

It could have stopped me from believing in others, and myself.

It could have affected my work ethic.

It could have meant no job promotions, and therefore no life coaching. No business. No clients. No growth. No soaring.

It could have meant not writing this book.

It could have meant not realising that I was never a black girl in the wrong suburb, just a young woman living her best life in a beautifully flawed world.

EDUCATION, EMPATHY, POSITIVITY, TOLERANCE

In Australia, I once gave a keynote presentation to a government department.

The rippled after-effects of this presentation were profound.

Members of the audience immediately put strategies in place to make departmental processes easier for refugees, stating that their existing approach was too black and white, and did not take into account individual circumstances and stories.

The reason they made such quick, positive changes is because they could see the hurdles refugees faced. It suddenly made sense to them why many refugees didn't have legal documentation such as birth certificates, drivers' licenses, and other legal papers— because often they'd fled their homeland quickly, sometimes with just the clothes they were wearing.

They also realised that refugees are desperate people taking extreme measures to leave difficult situations, and that they need extra support and understanding to help them build a new life in their new country.

Delivering this particular presentation was a standout defining moment, because it was the first time I really felt like I was a voice for the voiceless. My voice was listened to by open-minded, kind-hearted people who had the compassion and opportunity to make life easier for vulnerable individuals.

It was further proof that, when we understand each other and work together, we unite and flourish as a people, community, and country. What binds us is far greater than *anything* that separates us.

IMPORTANT REALISATIONS

When I started my business, something strange happened.

Clients would come into my office to have an initial meeting with me. The purpose of the meeting was to explore whether I should personally coach them, or whether I should refer them to one of my specialist coaches.

To do this, I'd need to ask them several questions. But often, the client wanted to ask *me* many of their own questions first. They'd hear my accent and wonder where I was from and why I left my country. They'd also wonder what I'd done in my life to be sitting opposite them as a business coach.

I understood their curiosity, and would often answer briefly before steering the conversation back to them. Sometimes my steering worked; other times it didn't. Either way, whether they persisted or not, the common recommendation in nearly every conversation was, 'You should write a book about your life.'

It was so funny and puzzling to me.

A book?

My life?

It seemed like such a strange proposition, and yet, not only did dozens of people suggest this, but investors wanted to be part of the project, believing my story could even be made into a movie.

Now *that* made me chuckle.

As humbling and surprising as all of this was, sharing my story was the last thing on my mind. If anything, I wanted to move *past* my past. I wanted to forget many of the traumatic memories and difficult journeys. I wanted to focus only on the present and the future. Also, the thought of baring my soul and personal life to strangers was absolutely terrifying.

But over the years, the chorus of people asking me to write the book became bigger, louder, and unrelenting.

Every time someone made the request, I briefly wondered why my story was so interesting, but didn't give any serious time or consideration to it ... until one day a little voice in my head said, 'Slow down; think about it.'

So I did.

I set aside a few hours one Saturday afternoon to ruminate and reflect. I started with some meditation to clear my mind, and then I implemented my A.R.T. framework to help me gain clarity.

I actually retraced the steps of my life journey, this time as a bystander, watching myself from afar. It's the first time I stopped long enough to realise what I'd actually done, gone through, and achieved.

I felt a humbled sense of pride and a deep well of gratefulness.

Yes, it became clear to me.

I realised that my story was no better or more remarkable than anyone else's, just inspiring in its own way.

I realised it was a story about overcoming adversity.

A story of courage and tenacity.

A story of hope.

I realised *many* other things too.

I realised that the sentiments and lessons in my own story could embody the sentiments and lessons in other people's stories as well, people who weren't in a position to write their own book.

I realised my story could be a practical tool to help others overcome obstacles, and defy their destiny. Because, while each of our problems might be different, our ways of overcoming them are the same—through awareness, questioning, courage, action, and perseverance.

I realised that my story could become a voice for the voiceless: refugees locked in detention centres craving freedom; child brides who simply want to enjoy their youth; women and men suffering in abusive relationships.

The more I thought about it, the more I realised my story could be the key that helps unlock happiness, freedom, and fulfilment.

When I realised *all* this, it truly was a defining, uplifting, and life-changing moment.

CONCLUSION

As this book draws to a close, I would like to thank you from the bottom of my heart for reading my story. I'd also like to reiterate some important messages.

Your harshest critic, and your biggest barrier, is probably you.

So let me say this: you *can* defy your destiny.

You *can* live the life of your choosing.

You *can* live a life of purpose and fulfillment.

Will it be easy? Probably not. But, how easy is your current life or your existing problems?

I've outlined my A.R.T. framework in Chapter Nine, which is a practical tool to help you defy your destiny.

However, if you ever want a quick strategy for on-the-go decision making, ask yourself these two simple questions:

One, what's wrong?

Two, how do I fix it?

It's as simple as that.

Just ask these questions, brainstorm ideas to improve the situation, and take action.

Don't look at the big, complicated picture—that can be too daunting and paralysing. Just look at the one, small step in front of you. The size of the step is irrelevant; the decision to make it, is enormous. It's that first step that will set you on the path to defying your destiny.

And remember, you don't have to be in extreme situations like mine. You can feel unfulfilled in your job, unsatisfied in a relationship, unhappy with your weight, unsure about your future, sick of smoking cigarettes, tired of your messy house. If you ignore any of these situations, you allow unhappiness to become your destiny for that moment in your life.

So, my friends ... *believe.*

You *can* and *will* defy your destiny with ideas and action.

Stay inspired.

Be emboldened.

Feel empowered.

You *can* do it!

I hope my story has reminded you that dreams are yours to dream, opportunities are yours to take, and mistakes are yours to make.

May you live the life you desire, the life you deserve, toward a destiny you determine.

ACKNOWLEDGEMENTS

I am grateful to many people in my life. Here, I would like to publicly thank them.

Thank you to my partner, Ben, for your unconditional love and support. You always amaze me with your goodness and genuineness. You are truly the backbone of our family.

Thank you to our son, Odis, for being the absolute love of our lives. Every time I look into your beautiful eyes, I feel inspired to be a better person. I feel driven to make a difference.

Thank you to Mum and Dad. I am alive and well because of your love and protection. I am a butterfly because of your cocoon.

Thank you to my brother, Amanuel, my soul mate. You were my guiding light when nearby, you are my guiding light while afar. This book is *our* book.

Thank you to my whole family and close friends. You've wrapped me in your warmth and showered me with wisdom. I shine because of your light.

Thank you to all my mentors. Your guidance and insight showed me the way, even if I sometimes used a different map.

Thank you to my investor, for your trust, belief, and action. You allowed me to tell my story in the way that was true for me. Your faith in this project is deeply appreciated.

Thank you to the many coaching clients I've worked with over the years, and the new clients I am yet to meet. I feel honoured to be part of your journeys.

Thank you to the wonderful women and men, boys and girls who have attended my keynote presentations. I am humbled by your presence, and amazed by your own stories.

Thank you to my professional writer. I had the story and many of the words, but you made those words sparkle. Thank you for ensuring that the last word was always mine.

Finally, thank you to YOU, dear reader. You invested time reading my story, and for that, I am beyond humbled. Now, I want to hear *your* story.

Please connect with me via all my social media channels, which you'll find on my website: www.fiorigiovanni.com